AY AND CONNECTIONS

METROPOLITAN RAILWAY
TUBE & DISTRICT RAILWAYS
OTHER RAILWAYS
GOLF COURSES

R. H. SELBIE.
GENERAL MANAGER

THE GOLDEN YEARS
OF THE
METROPOLITAN RAILWAY
and the Metro-land Dream

THE GOLDEN YEARS OF THE METROPOLITAN RAILWAY
and the Metro-land Dream

Dennis Edwards · Ron Pigram

BLOOMSBURY BOOKS
LONDON

Other titles in the Metro-land trilogy
by. Dennis Edwards and Ron Pigram
Metro Memories
Romance of Metro-land

Other titles in the transport series
The Final Link Dennis Edwards and
Ron Pigram
Midland Line Memories Brian Radford
Down the Line to Dover Muriel Searle

Illustrations
front cover: The cover of the 1930 *Metro-land* guide (*Robert Selbie's copy*)
back cover: The Junction at Aldgate in 1885. Metropolitan District railway Locomotive 26, a 4-4-0 tank, heads an Inner Circle train, while a Great Northern Railway 0-4-0 T comes up from Ludgate.
The afternoon goods train leaving Verney Junction with Metropolitan K class 2-6-4 T locomotive No. 115 on the last day of scheduled passenger operation, 4 July 1936. (*Stingemore Collection*)
endpapers: Metropolitan Railway Folder map showing the entire system in 1930.
frontispiece: Chiltern Court, the Metropolitan Railway's imaginative building in Baker Street, below which ran the trains to the Chiltern Hills. (Drawing by J. Harvey, 1924)

This edition published 1988 by
Bloomsbury Books an imprint of
Godfrey Cave Associates Limited
42 Bloomsbury Street, London WC1B 3QJ
under license from Baton Transport/
Cleveland Press

© Dennis Edwards & Ron Pigram 1983

ISBN 1 870630 11 4

Printed in Yugoslavia

ACKNOWLEDGEMENTS

The authors must, as in earlier books, record their sincere thanks to all those whose enthusiasm at talks and in correspondence has encouraged us to complete this three-volume work on the Metropolitan Railway's beloved Metroland. They have shown us that there are still many treasured memories, both in hearts and on gently fading prints, of those days. To all of you, may we say thank you for your help. We must also, as always, thank our many patient librarian friends, both in the London boroughs and at smaller libraries in Buckinghamshire and Hertfordshire.

We acknowledge illustrations from the following sources:
Charles E. Lee: 19(L), 27, 111(T)
London Transport: 15, 19(T), 22, 25, 30, 33(T), 32(L), 34(Y), 38, 43(L), 47, 49, 57(L), 62(T), 67(L), 68, 69(L), 72(T), 73(T), 79(L), 89(L), 90(T), 93(T), 101, 102(T), 104, 105(LT), 107(T), 110, 114, 116(T), 117(L), 118, 126(L)
Leicestershire Libraries and Museum service: 28, 36, 112(T)
North Hertfordshire Museum service: 28
Sigrist Collection: 31, 70(L), 93(L), 119(T)
Special L.T. collection: 32(Y), 34(L)
Mr A. Croughton: 36–37, 59, 65, 74(L), 78(L), 85(T), 98–99, 117(T)
Metro C W: 46(L), 68(T), 74(T)
Author's: frontispiece, 15–18, 33, 51–52(T), 56(T), 65(L), 66, 72(L), 73(L), 76, 88(T), 91, 92, 94–95, 102(L), 103(T), 106(T), 107, 108, 113(T), 116(L), 120(L), 121(L), 122(L), 126(T)
Private pamphlet: 43(L)
Michael Brookes: 48, 83(T), 84(T), 92(L)
Railway Magazine: 51(L), 53(T), 83(L)
Mr A. Geal: 56(L), 57(T), 71, 97(T)
Mr Borley: 61, 63, 64
Buckinghamshire County Museum: 80, 100
Pamlin Prints (Kenneth Carr): 81(L), 82
Buckinghamshire Libraries: 91(M)
F. Stingemore Collection: 109, 111(L), 115(T), 120, 121(T), 122(T)
Mr W. Atkinson: 39(T), 40–41, 44(L), 45(T)
London Borough of Hillingdon: 45(L), 67, 124
Miss A. Tugwell: 54, 75
LRGP: 123
Lower Birds Estate: 83
Mr Casserley: 113 (ex RMag), 127(T)
Alfred Hearn: 115
Mrs Bird: 119(L)

Contents

1 Come with us to Metro-land

To those with recollections of past years and a love of railway history, the name Metro-land brings moments of pure nostalgia. Perhaps all of us who love trains have a sneaking personal regard for the old Metropolitan Railway, which coined the name for its traffic area of the Chilterns. It was, after all, a unique railway, with such a personal pride in itself that it continued to regard itself as a main line company even after a setback to its ambitions in the 1920s, when the railway amalgamations did not include the 'Met'.

'Metro-land' will always embrace the ideals of fresh homes and pastures, of hope after the strains of war, of days out in the country with the wind in our faces and the sun tricking out all the wonders of nature in radiant gold, green and beechwood russet. The Chiltern Hills will always be there, but it was the Metropolitan Railway, all those years ago, that led Londoners out into the open air and took us home again.

Although we have, in our books *Romance of Metro-land* and *Metro Memories,* already traced the history of the Metropolitan Railway and its Metro-land dream, we make no apologies for turning around another time and, with the help of many well-wishers, collecting together some more material about those long-dead days between the two world wars – the days of the 'flappers' and wind-up gramophones, of coloured porch glass and 'semis' around the £800 mark, and of the power and smell of steam engines working the Chiltern banks with their loads of picnickers on a day out in the country. It is, after all, over fifty years since the Metropolitan Railway officially died, and over that half century we have seen the love of the Metro-land ideals live on and become a part of English history.

The Metropolitan was, of course, essentially a London railway, and it would be wrong to forget its origins as a practical means of solving mid-Victorian traffic problems. It was the world's first Underground railway, and the foundations laid down in the early 1860s were to provide London with transport for all, becoming enshrined as the Inner Circle of the Underground of today.

Although within twenty years the Metropolitan was actively looking outside its central London area of operation and towards opening up the meadow lands of north-west London, its original *raison d'être* may well have caused its demise. For the Metropolitan Railway, in spite of its 'main line' terminus of Baker Street (at one time Moorgate was proposed) was never able to lose its essential character as an Underground railway company. It was this aspect that drew it into the new monopoly of the London Passenger Transport Board in 1933.

All who are interested in the 'Met' and in Metro-land delight in the lovable paradoxes that the railway gave us. The most obvious was the idea that steam locomotives that had once worked in circles under London, like a giant toy railway set, could spend the last few years of their working lives out on an eccentric branch from Quainton Road junction to Brill, a little place buried in the remote Buckinghamshire countryside. Another was the contrast between the determined progress of the Metropolitan's electrifications of the early 1900s and the considerable steam locomotive capacity that took its trains northward from Rickmansworth. The Metropolitan Railway, as it proved with its Metro-land traffic advertising and promotional campaigns – which ran from the First World War with great persistence until the railway's death in 1933 – was an aggressive and determined organization, with enormous loyalty and *esprit de corps* among its staff. It was a product of its time, and its greatest hours came with the realization that leisure and happiness were marketable commodities that ordinary Londoners wanted and would strive to pay for. We shall not see its like again.

In this book, we examine a hundred years of the Metropolitan Railway and travel to the outermost limits of Metropolitan

Railway steam – the remote little crossing of the Oxford & Cambridge Railway line known as Verney Junction in the secret depths of rural Buckinghamshire. The photographs are those we have collected together since our first book was published, many of which have been kindly passed to us by generous readers who would like to share these historic scenes with others. Although some places, such as Brill, may appear to be unfairly over-represented, we have included as wide a range as possible, especially to help railway modellers who have over the years asked us to comment or help with the station layouts that have, for many decades, lain under the Buckinghamshire grass.

Ickenham and Hitchin
1983

2 The Metropolitan Railway

Early Years

As early as 1853 there was a scheme known as the Bayswater, Paddington and Holborn Bridge Railway on which the Metropolitan Railway was eventually based. By the time it received Parliamentary approval its title had changed to North Metropolitan Railway. The proposal was for a line from Paddington to King's Cross, and its promoters joined with the City Terminus Company which had sought to link Holborn with King's Cross. The project was incorporated as the Metropolitan Railway on 7 August 1854, and nine years later, on 10 January 1863, the first public trains with accommodation for first, second and third class passengers, ran between Bishop's Road, Paddington and Farringdon Street at about fifteen-minute intervals.

The service proved very popular in spite of the risks that such a novel method of railway transport implied. A locomotive boiler had already exploded with pyrotechnic force, and a large group of people was firmly convinced that the engine fumes would cause suffocation in the subterranean tunnels. Lighting was by flimsy gas bags feeding open lights to the compartments, and signalling was of the standard of the times.

Less than a year was to pass before the Metropolitan's success fuelled the promotion of other schemes; among those sanc-tioned was one to complete, with the District Railway, the completion of an Inner Circle, and another for a so-called outer circle by connection lines to existing railways. A fourth scheme of 1864 formed the basis of the Met's future ambitions – the Extension Line to Verney Junction via Aylesbury.

The Extension Line

Early records of the Metropolitan Railway of that time show that the Company was not in a sound financial condition, to put it mildly. The arrival of Sir Edward Watkin, who was already in control of two other railway companies, altered the policy and the fortunes of the Metropolitan Company. By the time the Inner Circle had been completed in 1884, Sir Edward had begun his schemes for an extension linking the Midlands and southern England by way of the Met's London lines (including the Widened Lines from King's Cross to Moorgate Street). During the next few years the Metropolitan Railway, pushing out into the Chilterns, established what was to become its 'Metroland'. The line from Harrow to Pinner opened in 1885, and Metropolitan trains reached Rickmansworth for the first time by 1887; the little town of Chesham was proud to receive its first 'Met' trains two years later.

The extension was rapidly car-ried forward, as the late Victorian prosperity made the railway link with London a vital one. A local line had already linked Verney Junction with Aylesbury, and when the 'Met' finally reached Aylesbury in 1894 the name of that far-flung outpost of the Metropolitan Railway's system could at last be carried on its trains from London (though at first the service was worked by local trains from Aylesbury).

The story of how the Metropolitan Railway and the Great Central Railway competed for traffic was described in the earlier books of this series. With the arrival of the Great Central in London, the Metropolitan Railway took over control of the line to Brill from the junction of Quainton Road in 1899. At one time there were plans to use this Brill line to extend rail services from London via the Chilterns to the outskirts of Oxford. Only when the proposals were dropped was the Brill Branch fated to wither and die.

The Metropolitan Railway sought constantly to increase its share of goods traffic in the area through which it ran, and its magnificent later locomotives of the 'H' and 'K' classes, built in the 1920s, were intended for freight duties. Coal traffic, including the supply of coal from the Midlands for the Met's own power station at Neasden via Verney Junction, were among the commodities transported by trains headed by these fine locomotives. The 'H' (4-4-4T) and the 'G' (0-6-4T) classes contrasted greatly with the Metropolitan's only two steam survivors today – an 'A' class 4-4-0 tank, built as long ago as 1864 (No. 23, which can be seen in the London Transport Collection at Covent Garden) and L44, an 'E' type, which is preserved at Quainton Road station site.

Metro-land

It was with the 1904 *Guide to the Extension Line* (a yearly publication that was to become timeless as the *Metro-land* guide, price one penny at station ticket offices) that a new leisure industry was born. Between the list of meetings of the local staghounds (for those Londoners who wished to take their own horses by Metropolitan Railway from London for a day's hunting) and a list of bed and breakfast accommodation at Brill and Wendover, was a group of country walks that could be undertaken. Walking (or hiking as it was known in the 1930s) and cycling soon became the most popular activities of Londoners on their day off work. Indeed, it was the glimpse of rural arcadia seen by many a young man who strolled the Chilterns with his lass over the next two decades that prompted many to become the Met's future customers – a house owner in Metro-land who travelled every day to his place of work in the City. Somehow, although the London inner country was rapidly swallowed up in a sea of new housing, the country areas of Metroland remained unspoilt, except for the occasional unsightly development outside the towns. Verney Junction and Brill, too far away from London even by Met, did not become intermediate towns on a railway system ruled from Baker Street, and slept the years away until the railway lines were finally weed-strewn and removed. The Metro-land dream had passed away.

3 Live in Metro-land

'Middlesex and Buckinghamshire have been closely allied with the rise and progress of the Metropolitan Railway. What a boon it has been to its myriad patrons . . . new towns and communities have been brought together. The Metropolitan is an organisation that does really care for the public in the spirit of service and with pride in their line . . . the Metropolitan Railway is the sustainer and creator of most of the centres on the line. The Metropolitan Railway's enterprise is unceasing and we are grateful for it.'

Middlesex Advertiser and Gazette
1923

To many people, Metro-land was synonymous with the growth of the north-western suburbs of London, particularly between the two wars. Yet the development of housing communities was a feature along the Metropolitan Extension Line long before the famous 'Metro-land' slogan appeared in 1915. Indeed, one of the earliest guide books to the Extension Line advertised houses at rustic Kilburn, and at Willesden Green to let for £70 a year.

By 1884, when the Metropolitan reached Northwood, then a hamlet in the northern part of the large parish of Ruislip, a local land developer, with the imposing name of Frank Murray Maxwell Hallowell Carew, was selling plots on a 767-acre estate near the new station. The houses were slow in coming, and even in 1890 passengers still had to ask the guard to

stop at Northwood.

The Metropolitan Railway went into the estate development business with the formation of the Metropolitan Surplus Lands Committee in 1885. Its first venture was at Pinner (the Cecil Park Estate), but it was the opening of the Harrow & Uxbridge Railway in 1904 that really launched the progress of Metro-land. At the official opening of the line on 30 June 1904 the Met's chairman stated that 'Some of those persons present here today would no doubt live to see the districts through which the new line passes develop and furnish homes for London's ever expanding population'. The Uxbridge newspaper commented: 'Uxbridge is expected to grow into a first-class residential neighbourhood and a health resort.'

One of the first development plans was the Ruislip–Northwood Garden City project, which the local council promoted under the Housing and Planning Act of 1909. It was the first local authority in the country to do so. A competition was held for a development based on Ebenezer Howard's Letchworth Garden City. A. & J. Soutar's Ruislip plans were exhibited in London and drew favourable comment. The backbone of the plan was a tree-lined road from South Ruislip (then called Northolt Junction, on the GW/GCR Joint Line) to Northwood, with a series of squares, lakes and housing and

shopping groups. Ruislip Manor Limited was formed to carry out the project, but only a few properties were built before the First World War came to change everything. Ruislip Manor station opened in 1912 to serve the projected estate.

The Metropolitan was keen to promote growth around its stations. But the middle-class clerks of pre-1914 London were unable to afford the fairly high fares, nor was there a proper financial and estate development structure to help home owners on lower incomes at that time. It was the managerial classes to which the pre First World War Met publicity appealed: 'The strains which the London business or professional man has to endure amongst the turmoil and bustle of town can only be counter-balanced by the quiet restfulness and comfort of a residence in pure air and rural surroundings.'

Following the launch of *Metro-land* in 1915, the Metropolitan's publicity department became increasingly active and soon the term 'Metro-land' became part of London life. An enterprising music publisher brought out a 'Vocal One-Step' called 'My Little Metro-land Home', with words by Boyle Lawrence and music by Henry Thraile. The slogan 'Live in Metro-land' was even engraved on the inside door-plates of the Watford Line compartment stock trains. And Evelyn Waugh had a Margot Metro-land in one of his novels.

Robert H. Selbie, the Metropolitan's brilliant and enterprising general manager, stated in 1912 that the Metropolitan was not getting its proper benefits from the Surplus Lands Committee. He suggested to the Committee the formation of a separate estates development company. 'The area which the Metropolitan serves is daily growing in popularity and the experience of some of the house and estate agents is that they cannot supply the demand for houses at rentals between £41 and £100 per year,' he stated.

At the end of the First World War Selbie reported: 'In view of the large demand there will be for houses as soon as Peace is declared and the Forces are demobilized, and also in view of the advertisement the districts (served by the Metropolitan) have received during the War, I am of the opinion that the scheme should be taken in hand forthwith.' Selbie felt his mission was to provide houses fit for heroes to live in – provided that they could put down the deposit with their demobilization gratuity and keep up the monthly payments!

The Metropolitan Railway Country Estates Company was formed in 1919, with a starting capital of £150,000, later increased to £200,000. The Metropolitan

Railway did not hold shares, but could elect the chairman. The offices of the Estates Company were at Baker Street station; H. Gibson was appointed estate agent, and the full resources of the Met's publicity department were at the disposal of the Estates Company. An important objective of the company was 'to combine to their fullest extent all that is beautiful in housing architecture with the natural beauties of the site'. The first land purchased was at Chalk Hill, Wembley Park (123 acres for £32,500, with further additions of over forty acres at Kingsbury for £11,683). The Cedars estate at Rickmansworth was bought for £40,000 and comprised some forty-five acres.

A press announcement said: 'The Metropolitan Railway Country Estates has been originated not merely to provide superior houses in the rural countryside near London, but also to create new passenger traffic.' The pages of *Metro-land* were filled with advertisements for the estates at Woodcock Hill (Kenton), Ruislip (Manor Farm, Eastcote Road), Hillingdon, Pinner, Amersham, etc. The development of Metroland was well under way by the mid 1920s.

The 1930s saw the Golden Age of the housing estates. Row upon row of semi-detached and detached houses and bungalows in variations of mock Tudor began to spread out

beside the Metropolitan Railway lines. Houses with stained glass windows on the landing and in the hall; houses with coal or coke boilers in the kitchen and fitted kitchen cabinets; electric light shades in every room – there were all kinds of inducements to persuade people to move out of inner London to a brave new world amid the elms and clay fields of Middlesex. Here the birds sang and the milkman with his horse and cart delivered twice a day. There were golf courses and parks; country walks and old villages like Pinner and Ruislip, and a house with a garden already dug and, in some cases, turf lawns laid.

These are just some of the many advertisements that appeared in Metro-land publications:

Ruislip: Houses from £750 . . . a kitchen with every modern requirement . . . a treasure for the housewife. (1937)
Kingsbury, Jenning's Estate: Every house is a show house. (1933)
Eastcote, Comben and Wakeling: Eastcote Park Estate . . . £975 distinctive residences.
Eastcote, London's latest ideal and picturesque residential district is now being developed by the well-known builders T.F. Nash. Detached and semi-detached houses in a variety of designs, £895–£1150.
Ickenham, R.T. Warren houses in

the Swakeleys Estate: In truly rural settings for only 22/6d a week. *Hillingdon:* A house, a garage and a garden can be yours for £5 down (MRCE's Hillingdon Mount Estate). The nearby Highfields Estate was advertised: Ample garden space so as to ensure for all time spaciousness and privacy. *Ruislip,* A.L. Bowers Ruislip Station Estate, 1933: An estate that's definitely different. Lose no time in paying the estate a visit – for the dream house you have yearned for is waiting . . . ready to be secured for a price easily within your reach.

On 29 August 1929 an historic event took place in the muddy meadows near Rayners Lane halt. The first sod was turned on what was to be the Metropolitan Railway Country Estates' first venture into lower priced housing: Harrow Garden Village Estate. The builder was E.S. Reid, who had at one time been Director of Highways for Harrow Council. Mr Reid paid for extra sidings to be put down beside the line just by Rayners Lane bridge on the Harrow side, so that building supplies could be brought direct to the estate.

'A new township is to rise on land where from time immemorial there has been nothing but farms and fields. An army of labourers is at work on the new arterial road to North Harrow,' said the local press. E.S. Reid's publicity en-

thused: 'This beautifully laid out, well timbered estate of over 213 acres, with 16 acres of permanent open space, recreation grounds and tennis courts, adjoins Rayners Lane station and is within 11 miles of Baker Street, which is reached by over 200 trains daily. There are plans for 1600 houses and 240 shops.' (1931)

Just south of Rayners Lane station, A. Robinson began housing operations: 'An £850 house for £750 . . . by cutting profits, mass purchase of materials, team methods and painstaking care.'

The popularity of Rayners Lane was enormous, particularly after T.F. Nash ('builder of over 4000 houses in Harrow; 1000 men employed in 1934') began his vast estate of over twenty roads to the south of Rayners Lane. 'The talk of the town' – with row upon row of semi-detached and terraced houses from £595. 'Free electric light fittings and nicely designed, tree planted footpaths.' The estate soon spread neo-Tudor houses right across the old flat fields towards Eastcote Lane.

By July 1934 there was something to shout about, and Nash erected a temporary triumphal archway over the main shopping street, with the words 'THE SUMMIT OF HIGH VALUE'. Nash advertised his estates: 'An effort to get away from old ideas and monotony'. The irony was unintentional, but today there can be few suburbs as

uninteresting and as devoid of wide open spaces than the southern half of Rayners Lane.

In November 1931 E.S. Reid celebrated the rise of Harrow Garden Village with a great fireworks display to which Londoners could travel on the Met at reduced fares. A similar display was held at Ruislip Manor on 6 October 1933. George M. Ball's Manor Homes, similar in design to the Rayners Lane Nash estate (the companies were closely related), were launched with a great spectacular attracting 20,000 people. The BBC made one of its rare outside broadcasts, and the London *Evening News* offered coupons for cheap fare. The set firework pieces included the words in fire 'REMEMBER MANOR HOMES'. There was a nostalgic and at the same time foreboding note, for one set piece depicted a Zeppelin coming down in flames.

By the end of the year well over 2500 homes were under construction at Ruislip Manor, sweeping like a tide that had no ebb over the flat lands towards Northolt Junction.

The year 1933 had other significance: London Transport came into being and absorbed the reluctant Metropolitan Railway. It was the peak year of suburban building. Rayners Lane station was handling 22,000 passengers. By the end of 1937, the total was four million. A temporary station was erected, to be replaced in 1938 by one of Holden's classic red brick and concrete structures. The new building became the hub of modern Rayners Lane. The tall windows of the station's great red-brick tower were illuminated at night to look like a temple guiding the pleasure-seeker to the delights of the West End.

The opening of the Grosvenor (later Odeon) Cinema at Rayners Lane in 1936, with its sweeping Art Deco concrete façade, put Rayners Lane on the map as an ultra-modern suburb. Here suburban housewives, with free time on their hands now that they lived in 'labour saving homes,' could weep away a Wednesday afternoon watching the latest Clark Gable film. Afterwards, they could repair their ravaged faces in the luxurious 'Hollywood-style cosmetic room for the convenience of lady patrons'. Then they could relax in the tea lounge, where uniformed waitresses served tea in square cups and Lyons cakes on square plates. On Friday nights the family could see the newest films, plus 'three live cabaret acts straight from the West End'. Rural Metro-land was a distant memory.

Completely new districts grew up in these years. Northwood Hills began in May 1930, when local businessman Norman Peachey began to develop, with a builder called Harry Neale, the area of fields along the road between Pin-

ner Green and Northwood at a point where muddy Joel Street came up from Eastcote. The local press held a competition to find a name for the new area. Ruislip–Northwood Council favoured 'Northwood Town', but the press and the Metropolitan Railway organized the competition. The prize was £5 and the paper promised that 'no envelope will be open before 27 March 1933'. A lady from North Harrow won, with the name 'Northwood Hills'.

A similar competition was held for a new station to be opened between Kingsbury and Canons Park on the new Stanmore branch. The result was the not very imaginative 'Queensbury'. The district was probably the most rapidly growing of all Metro-land suburbs. Thousands of houses, shopping parades and light manufacturing units covered the area north of Kingsbury by the end of the 1930s.

By the late 1930s the old Metro-land of country walks, tea gardens and pioneering housing estates was over. A poignant note was struck by a correspondent in the *Middlesex Advertiser and Gazette* (Uxbridge) in 1937, when he wrote that while travelling on the 11.40 a.m. train from Eastcote to Rayners Lane he noticed a cock pheasant flying alongside the train. 'This would have been a common sight less than eight years ago, but a rarity now,' he recalled.

The Metropolitan Railway

created a whole new world, but in doing so it destroyed for ever acres of beautiful countryside and a way of life that was quiet, peaceful and essentially English.

By the end of the 1930s, common sense saw that the ever-flowing tide of London expansion had to be stopped. The Green Belt and the Second World War saw to that. When the sirens sounded and the sandbags came out, the dream of Metro-land was finally over.

4
The Pioneers
1863 to 1904
From dreams to reality

Early Plans and Railway schemes

Early plans and railway schemes: A plan for an underground railway system, which would have run in open conduit just below street level, was published as part of the report by the Select Committee on Metropolitan Communications of 1855. The Great Exhibition of 1851 had encouraged architectural schemes linking the City area by railway, and Charles Pearson, the City solicitor, advocated ways of bringing the broad gauge railway trains into the heart of the metropolitan area.

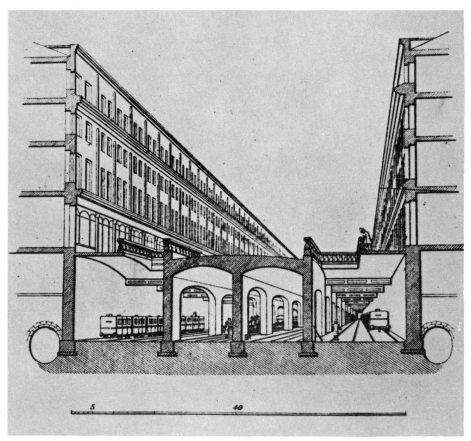

This sketch shows how the railway would have been designed as an integral part of a very broad new roadway system, flanking the houses and new sewer systems.

Another proposal was for widened or new streets to run between the two lines of underground openings that allowed steam to escape. The apertures would have been protected only by stone panelling.

Pearson's scheme for a railway along the Fleet valley would have acted as a link for railways then under development in the north of London. The scheme became, in 1851, the City Terminus Company. The broad gauge tracks were seen, in future years, to have connected with Paddington. This plan of the proposed railway provides for an extension of Victoria Street, with railways below, to link with the Great Northern Railway at King's Cross. Its southern terminus at Farringdon was at the point reached by the Metropolitan Railway's first trains a decade later.

The terminus railways scheme would have required considerable levelling work, almost filling in the area of Holborn Hill. One problem with underground excavations in the heart of the City at the time was the presence of old graveyards. When the Midland Railway's St Pancras terminal was being built in 1866 one gentleman ratepayer complained of the 'horrible stench' that residents nearby experienced when the pauper section of the old burial ground there was exposed; some skulls and bones had been unearthed and had been thrown, higgledy-piggledy, all over the ground.

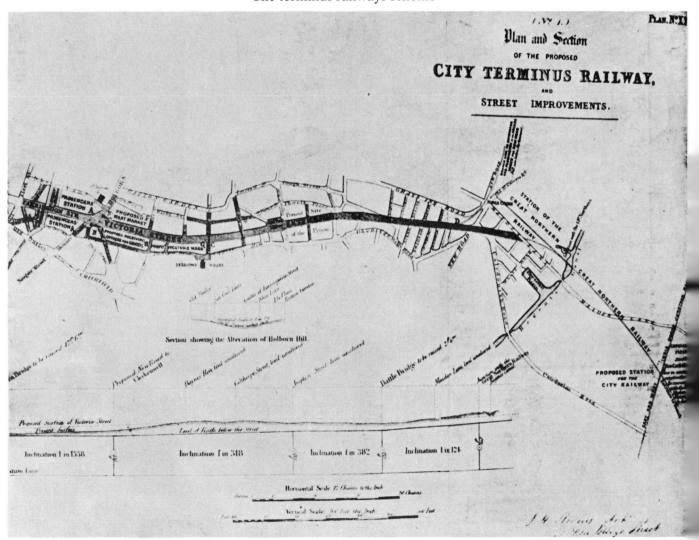

This illustration from the *Illustrated Times* of October 1861 shows that the work of lifting the excavated earth to the surface was assisted by a primitive machine.

An old print showing the excavation of the Metropolitan Railway tunnels at King's Cross in the early 1860s. The multiple brick rings of the subterranean arches can be seen at the far end of the timber shoring. Part of an unfinished cutting near Tunbridge Place fell in on 24 May 1861, carrying away pavements and gas mains.

How the Met grew. These six sketch maps show how the Metropolitan Railway and the Metropolitan District Railway grew between 1863 and 1884, when the Inner Circle was finally completed. They are especially interesting as they show the alterations to original station names.

The line to Hammersmith was promoted by a separate company known as the Hammersmith & City Railway (a name preserved with the Line). It was to build from Westbourne Park to Hammersmith, with a branch at Latimer Road (first known as Ladbroke Road) to the Uxbridge Road. This was worked broad gauge until the Met took over the service with standard stock on April 1865. An Act of 1864 had allowed the extension from Paddington to South Kensington; another Act of that year gave the go-ahead for a line from Moorgate to Tower Hill. The Metropolitan District Railway (the District) was granted the remainder of London's Inner Circle Line – from South Kensington to Tower Hill. The Metropolitan & St John's Wood railway, partly owned by the Met, opened a single line linking Baker Street to Swiss Cottage in April 1868. Friction between the two main London underground companies prevented the completion of the Inner Circle until 1884. On the first day, Metropolitan trains ran on the Outer rail, and District trains on the Inner.

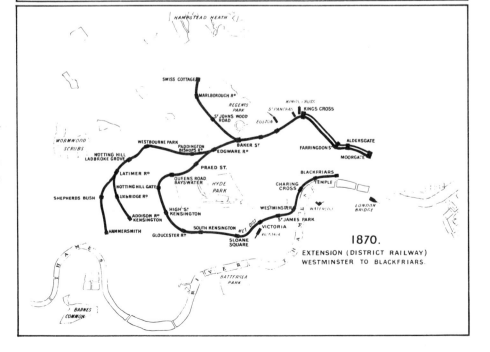

1863.
BISHOPS ROAD TO FARRINGDON STREET.

1864.
EXTENSION TO HAMMERSMITH

1870.
EXTENSION (DISTRICT RAILWAY)
WESTMINSTER TO BLACKFRIARS.

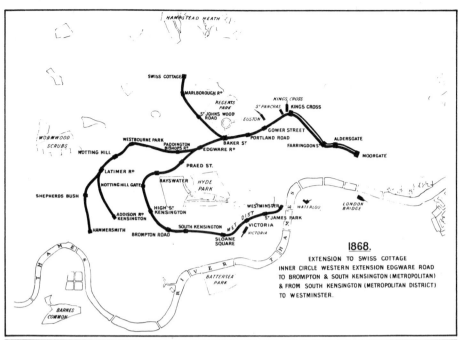

1868.

EXTENSION TO SWISS COTTAGE
INNER CIRCLE WESTERN EXTENSION EDGWARE ROAD
TO BROMPTON & SOUTH KENSINGTON (METROPOLITAN)
& FROM SOUTH KENSINGTON (METROPOLITAN DISTRICT)
TO WESTMINSTER.

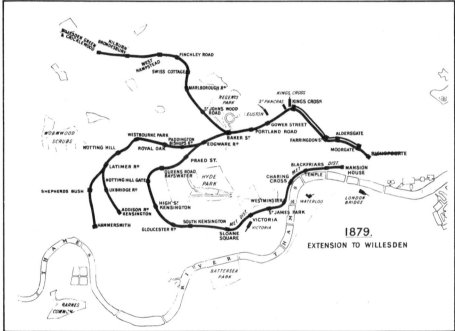

1879.

EXTENSION TO WILLESDEN

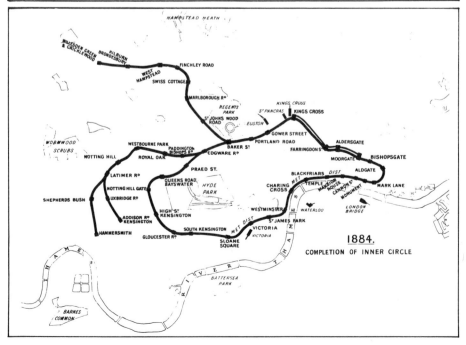

1884.

COMPLETION OF INNER CIRCLE

A train leaving the entrance to Clerkenwell Tunnel in 1868, showing the 'widened lines' from King's Cross passing under the original lines. Much of the railway between King's Cross and Farringdon Street was in open cutting, and the 728-yard-long tunnel was the only real tunnel on the original line.

Balance sheet: The Metropolitan Railway's first General Statement upon opening the Line, showing receipts and payments to June 1863. Note the item for 'omnibus subsidies' and the outstanding payment for carrying Great Western traffic.

THE METROPOLITAN RAILWAY COMPANY.

Dr.   GENERAL STATEMENT OF RECEIPTS AND PAYMENTS TO 30th JUNE, 1863.   Cr.

CAPITAL ACCOUNT.

	£ s. d.	£ s. d.		£ s. d.	£ s. d.	£ s. d.
To Amount received on Share Capital to 31st December, 1862	842,251 0 0		By Total Expenditure reported to 31st December, 1862		1,329,296 2 3	
Ditto from 1st January, 1863, to 30th June	5,249 0 0	847,500 0 0	Purchase of Lands	90,346 9 7		
Amount received on Preference Capital of £300,000 to 31st December, 1862	63,833 0 0		Works	32,699 17 4		
Ditto from 1st January, 1863, to 30th June	173,570 0 0	237,403 0 0	Parliamentary and Engineering (Finsbury Extension)	5,483 10 8		
Amount received on Extension Capital of £500,000		180,478 0 0	Interest on Debentures due 15th January, 1863	8,454 9 0		
Amount received on Debenture Bonds at 5 per Cent.	7,110 0 0		Dividend on Preferential Shares on 30th December, 1862	871 17 2		
" " " 6 per Cent.	275,890 0 0	283,000 0 0	Interest on Loans and Calls paid in advance	5,097 10 7		
Retention Fund on Contract for Works		12,442 10 0	Office Expenses £1,268 1 4			
			Directors, Auditors, &c. 979 6 9			
				2,247 8 1		
			Less ⅓rd charged to Revenue 749 2 8			
				1,498 5 5	144,451 19 9	
						1,473,748 2 0
			Balance:—			
			Cash deposited with Accountant-General 32,000 0 0			
			Cash at Bankers 55,075 8 0			
						87,075 8 0
		£1,560,823 10 0				£1,560,823 10 0

REVENUE ACCOUNT.

	£ s. d.	£ s. d.		£ s. d.	£ s. d.
To Amount received from Great Western Company on account	16,000 0 0		By Proportion of Office Expenses, Directors' Fees, &c.	749 2 8	
Ditto for Interest on Balance and Calls	689 18 9		Omnibus Subsidies	39 0 0	
Ditto for Rents	2,307 9 1		Interest on Debentures due 15th July	8,454 9 0	
Ditto for Transfer Fees	430 5 0				9,242 11 8
Premiums on sale of 6,000 Preference Shares	3,750 0 0	23,177 12 10	Dividend on Preference Shares at 5 per cent. per annum		4,215 0 0
			Ditto on £847,500 original Capital at 5 per cent. per annum		21,187 10 0
Undetermined Balance of Account due from Great Western Company for the Traffic carried by them over the Railway, estimated upon the basis of the Heads of Arrangement, say	16,500 0 0		Balance carried to next Half Year's Account		5,032 11 2
		£39,677 12 10			£39,677 12 10

Audited, save as regards the estimated balance of £16,500, or thereabouts, due from the Great Western Company for traffic receipts.

August 18th, 1863.

BENJ. JNO. ARMSTRONG. } Auditors.
SAMPSON COPESTAKE.

A crowded compartment. Travelling by Underground in the 1890s was quite unpleasant, but the Metropolitan Railway was said to carry nearly a hundred million passengers each year, the majority of whom 'accept the idea of tunnel travelling as easily as buying a newspaper'.

The *Windsor Magazine* of 1897 reported, with a foretaste of a perennial topic of discussion on underground travel, that 'the Companies running the Inner Circle offer a magnificent leading line in penny fares. In fact the work of the Directors is beyond praise. They have reduced all fares to such a low tariff that, were it not for unreasonable and extortionate shareholders, the day surely would not be far distant when the public would be asked to travel for nothing.'

Advertisements on platforms, together with the constant fug from the locomotives, made the work of discovering the name of the station from the bleary windows of the carriage very difficult. The advertising was so ubiquitous that jokers suggested that porters' uniforms could be labelled with favourite brands of medicinal remedies over 'the appropriate parts'.

Some of the Inner Circle stations had 'moveable signals' on the platforms giving a complete list of stations at which the approaching train would call. Another useful device of those days was the marking of tickets with a larger letter I (or O) – presumably standing for Inner or Outer rail – and for large signboards at the platforms proclaiming:

ALL TICKETS MARKED

I (or O)

THIS WAY →

In spite of this, few passengers were prepared to enter a train without confirming its destination with a porter; a railway employee who found tempers rapidly at breaking point in the smoky darkness.

Another early feature of station life in the Victorian tunnels was the penny-in-the-slot weighing machine. Every station had one. They were really large balances fitted with red velvet cushions and were popular with old gentlemen who secured a comfortable seat while waiting for a train.

Watching the patent indicator. This sketch of a Circle train in the 1890s shows an attempt to advise passengers in the compartment carriages of the next station. It worked in a rather crude mechanical way, being operated by a flap of wood projecting between the tracks and positioned a short way into the tunnel. Upon leaving the station, the carriages passed over the projection, which struck a spring at the bottom of each compartment that worked the carriage indicator. It was the guard's duty to report upon their effectiveness and to reset the indicators, by means of a cord, at the terminus. The Metropolitan Railway proved not in favour of full installation.

Let's all go down the Strand by one of the Metropolitan's three horse buses, seen here at Charing Cross in the 1890s. The umbrellas were purple and bore the name Metropolitan Railway. The services ran across London between Metropolitan stations, beginning in August 1866 and lasting until September 1901.

This sketch, from early Metropolitan Railway records, was designed to show the improvements in signalling during fifty years, but the design has been scrawled through and an earlier introduction date given for the automatic signal. The signalman of the 1860s must have had the worst job on the underground railway, for within a few years trains ran every few minutes. It would seem to have been a lowly position: 'I started as a signalman and am now responsible for the whole station,' said one station inspector in the 1890s.

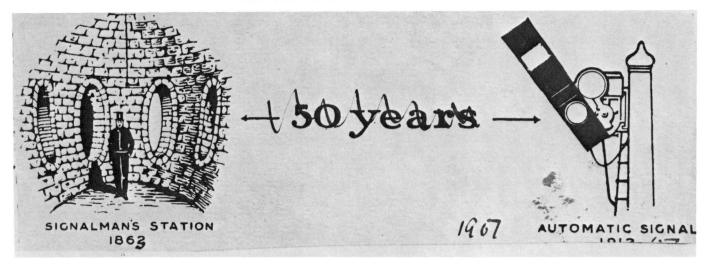

SIGNALMAN'S STATION 1863

1967

AUTOMATIC SIGNAL

A typical guard, like the one here, reached his position by working through lower grades, including porter and in the early days signalman. He was a senior member of the operating crew. In steam days station porters worked two shifts – from 5 a.m. to 3 p.m. and from 3 p.m. until 1 a.m. A porter took a hand at everything: lamp trimming and filling, engine coupling and closing all the individual doors of a train. (Readers who can recall the last compartment stock on the Metropolitan line in the early 1960s will remember the thunderous clanging of dozens of compartment doors before the train could depart.)

Newsboys were allowed inside the stations to sell papers. They were on their pitches from six in the morning until six at night. A nosey philanthropist asked one of them about the long day and was told: 'I don't know; it's cold at times, but it's better than being on the streets.' The newboys were paid 6s. (30p) a week.

Theatre traffic. This sketch in the *Windsor Magazine* gives a graphic glimpse of the limitations of underground steam railways. Here at King's Cross well-to-do theatre crowds, dressed in the height of fashion, wait on the ordinary board platform as the locomotive approaches, belching gasps of steam and sulphur into the air that turn around the lights and drop in smutty globules upon the throng at the back about to enter. London in the 1890s had so much to attract the crowds; the plays of Oscar Wilde sparkled in the early years of that decade while the odd and the unusual also helped to increase railway receipts. One such an occasion took place in March 1889, when Miss Anna Swann appeared from America to captivate the London scene. She was not an actress but a young woman over 8ft. 1in. in height who, when seated, was taller than other ladies standing. 'One cannot help thinking that marriage with such a gigantic specimen of loveliness would be a modified form of bigamy' rhapsodized one star-struck journalist upon seeing the creature.

WOTTON TRAMWAY.

RAILWAY CLEARING HOUSE.

ABSTRACT of all ~~TRAFFIC other than~~ PASSENGERS CARRIED by PASSENGER TRAIN.

Forwarded from _____ to _____ on the _____ Railway,

Via _____ For the Month of _December_ 188_8_

McCorquodale & Co., Limited, Cardington Street, London, N.W.

The Wotton Tramway. Far away, in rural Buckinghamshire, the Duke of Buckingham and Sir Harry Verney, two of the county's most illustrious landowners, were deeply involved with railway developments that were originally seen as providing transport for their local farm produce and estate workers. The Wotton Tramway was a light railway for Buckingham's estate, and was created in 1870 by ordinary local labour, no contractors being employed, although the actual lines were professionally laid. The line from Aylesbury to the junction station at Claydon (named Verney Junction in honour of Sir Harry Verney), was opened in September 1868. Both stretches of railway were to become part of the Metropolitan Railway system, and to feature in the *Metro-land* guides. The Wotton Tramway was, however, a very rural farm railway in the nineteenth century, though it was tied in to the Railway Clearing House system, as this abstract of passengers carried during December 1888 shows. The Wotton Tramway was interesting for the several 'sidings' which led off to gasworks, brickworks, and a remote farm and coal shunt on the Kingswood Lane. This latter 'branch' was laid down about the time of the tramway to Brill, but was always used for agricultural purposes. Most of the rails (except the last ¼ mile) were lifted in 1915, twenty years before the Metropolitan (by then London Transport) was to abandon the Brill Branch.

In October 1894, just over five years before the Metropolitan Railway took over the working of the Brill Branch (Wotton Tramway), the little branch line to Brill was taken over by the Oxford & Aylesbury Tramway Company, which relaid the original track. There had been talk of extending the line to Oxford itself and the city name had been included in the name of the company. (This was without doubt an attraction to the Metropolitan Railway's directors, who were at about this time looking at ways to extend the area of operations.) The Oxford proposals,

The sower. This interesting old print shows the method of scattering seed in the Chilterns at the end of the last century. This happy labourer, stoutly shod, is broadcast sowing from this sectioned seed tray. The knack, obviously, was to cast as evenly as possible, and he stares resolutely ahead.

providing for halts at farms and by-roads between Brill and Oxford, were soon abandoned, but this sketch, based on a little-known *Cycling and Touring Guide* of 1894, indicates the possible route by which Oxford could have been reached from Baker Street. The line would have required a tunnel under Muswell Hill, west of Brill station. This would have been the main factor in the abandonment of the scheme.

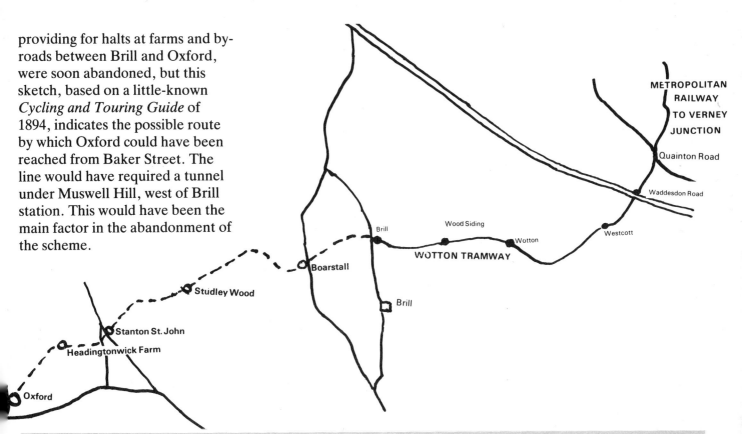

A junction in the course of being built. This scene shows the construction of the great Central Railway's new main line to London at a point near its link with the Metropolitan Railway's line from Verney Junction, over the embankment on the left. A new rounded arch bridge has just been built for the Great Central, and final adjustments are being made by the lengthmen, watched by curious schoolchildren.

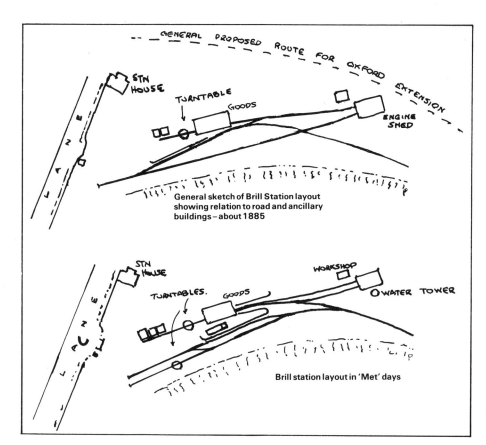

General sketch of Brill Station layout
showing relation to road and ancillary
buildings – about 1885

Brill station layout in 'Met' days

This sketch of the station layout at Brill shows the altered arrangement from the early days to the position during the Met era. The locomotive shed and the goods shed are shown in illustrations in this book. The proposed extension to Oxford was planned to sweep around the old station complex. The first sketch is based on early Ordnance maps.

Met 'A' class locomotives shown in this early print are No. 4 and No. 14, built by Beyer Peacock from 1864. They are shown here with clerestory-roofed stock at Hammersmith sheds. The Hammersmith Branch had opened on 13 June 1864, and used the Great Western railway lines between Bishop's Road and Westbourne Park. Great Western rolling stock had at first been used, and the branch was run as a Metropolitan and Great Western Committee line. This association with the

Great Western continued into London Transport days, when travel by its employees over this section of line was restricted.

The first eighteen locomotives, of which two are shown here, were originally named as follows (engine No. 1 was scrapped December 1897 after a collision):

1	Jupiter	10	Cerberus
2	Mars	11	Latona
3	Juno	12	Cyclops
4	Mercury	13	Daphne
5	Apollo	14	Dido
6	Medusa	15	Aurora
7	Orion	16	Achilles
8	Pluto	17	Ixion
9	Minerva	18	Hercules

Mr A. Hearn of Charlbury has suggested to us that the unusual names selected for these locomotives, in accord with mid-Victorian ideals of grandeur, also have a close resemblance to the titles of paintings exhibited in the Titian Gallery at Blenheim Palace at the time the locomotives were being built. The entire gallery at Blenheim Palace was destroyed by fire in February 1861 and was reported in *Jackson's Oxford Journal* of that year. The paintings reported lost in the flames were of Mars and Venus, Cupid and Psyche, Apollo and Daphne, Pluto and Prosperine, Hercules and Deganira, Vulcan and Ceres, Bacchus and Ariadne, Jupiter and Juno, and Neptune and Amphitrite.

Not all the names chosen for the locomotives were identical to those of the paintings, but it is significant that there are eighteen names in both cases and the likeness is obvious. It could well be that the publicity given to the loss of the paintings at the time suggested the names of these Greek gods and goddesses for the modern leviathans.

Metropolitan veteran No. 3, one of the original Class 'A' locomotives that were built from 1864, specially fitted with a steam pump and associated tubing on the front buffer. These pumps, which were used to deal with flooded areas of underground track, could handle 700 gallons a minute. The small vent, directly in line with the piping reaching down from the stack, is the steam escape. No. 26 was another locomotive fitted for flood works; an illustration of it in action may be seen in *Romance of Metro-land*. During the terrific storm on 6 May 1915 a sewer under the Widened Lines broke near Farringdon Street on the Met, and the low-level tunnel under the electric lines filled with water.

The Victoria Embankment, beneath which the complete Inner Circle was to run within two years of this picture being taken in 1882. The Embankment was started as early as 1864 (London in the 1860s must have been one glorious traffic jam!) but progress was delayed when the District railway was authorized for construction alongside it, and this caused the abandonment of a proposed dock at the eastern end of the Embankment. The railway paid £200,000 towards the cost of construction of the line from Westminster Bridge to Mansion House. The Embankment was formed not on the actual bank of the river but on a strip of foreshore (varying from 200 feet to 450 feet in width) that was reclaimed from the river. The young plane trees along the walkway were the first to be planted in a thoroughfare of this importance.

A train on the Inner Circle about 1870. This rear view of the compartment stock used on the Inner Circle shows the iron steps used to reach the roof. When trains first ran, lighting was supplied to two jets in the first class compartments and to one jet to the second and third classes, from gas bags arranged along the centre of the train roof. Compressed oil gas was used after 1877 and the gas was stored in cylinders (note the train to the right). Incidentally, the square-topped doors shown in this picture were replaced in stock built after 1867 by the traditional Metropolitan rounded top door, which persisted until the 1960s. The rounded doors were to lessen the danger from doors flying open in tunnels.

The Metropolitan tended to use long names for its stations. Just look at the name-board in this picture of 'Aldersgate Street and Barbican'. The high roof of the station was damaged during the Second World War in a massive night attack on the City. The roof was removed in the 1950s.

Snow falls in the buffet of Aldersgate
                                    Station,
Toiling and doomed from Moorgate
                          Street puffs the train,
For us of the steam and the gaslight,
                                the lost generation,
The new white cliffs of the City are
                                    built in vain.

*Sir John Betjeman: 'Monody on the death
of Aldersgate Street Station'*

Marlborough Road was one of the stations on the original single tracked St John's Wood Railway, and it was here that the lunch to celebrate the line's opening was held in 1868. 'The railway is constructed as a single line at present, with double lines at stations. Provision is made for a double line extension towards Hampstead', said a contemporary report. The railway became the route by which the Metropolitan broke out of the 'iron ring which the larger railway companies had built round it', and extended into Middlesex and Buckinghamshire. The station closed on 18 November 1939, when the Bakerloo Tube was extended to Finchley Road and Stanmore. The building is now a restaurant.

There are so many signs at Wood Lane station on the Metropolitan and GWR line to Hammersmith that it is difficult to find the ticket office, let alone the trains. Though 'Wood Lane (Exhibition) station is most conveniently situated in the grounds of the exhibition and is connected thereto by a covered way'. Wood Lane and White City were the great centres for international exhibitions before the First World War.

A look at what is was like at King's Cross at street level. This turn-of-the-century picture shows a variety of vehicular traffic, including a horse tram (plying between Hampstead and Holborn), a railway delivery cart (No. 506) in the foreground, a hansom cab, a horse bus and a spare pair of wheels! No motor cars – but a lady pushes an iron pram before the sandwich-board man who appears to be advertising a London theatre. Below, on the Underground, it was all going on as well.

Town planning was a thing of the future when this photograph was taken of the old station at Edgware Road. The building was replaced in the 1920s and the station re-formed with two island platforms, ready for the abortive plan to build tunnels under Edgware Road to provide a relief line for the main Metropolitan route from Finchley Road to Baker Street. The relief line would have joined the main line between Kilburn and Willesden Green. The indicators on the new Edgware Road station had destinations such as Uxbridge, Aylesbury and Verney Junction (which remained until the 1950s)! Part of the lettering high on the wall in the right of this picture was still visible seventy years later.

Aylesbury in about 1899, with No. 77 'E' class locomotive and a Baker Street train. This locomotive was built at Neasden in 1896 to the designs of the Metropolitan's chief mechanical engineer, T.F. Clark. Note the early form of Metropolitan insignia on the engine. This locomotive had a very long life and was not withdrawn until 1962.

The carriage is one of the 'Jubilee' four-wheel series of 1887, built for the Extension Line. The guard's compartment (window nearest engine) could be used in rush periods for passengers. They were accommodated on wooden seats. The 'Jubilee' stock lasted until 1912.

One day on the 1890s somebody with a strong political view felt that he could advance his cause by providing a black bag loaded with lethal fireworks. This was the result. The carriage (one of the rigid eight-wheelers, believed to be number 93) stands in ruins at Neasden. The explosion took place near Paddington (Praed Street).

Last resting place of the early Metropolitan Railway stock. This photograph was taken in September 1960 at the village of Lacanan Médoc vers Bordeaux, on the Ligne du Blayais Meseau des Landes de la Girade and the Ligne Lacanan à l'Océan. The only alteration to the coaches was the addition of an inside corridor. Note the double-stepped running boards.

The north junction at Harrow, showing the tracks to Uxbridge before the current rails were laid. The houses on the far right were then new and marked the edge of Harrow town.

When the contract was obtained by Bott & Stennett for building the line to Uxbridge, Walter Atkinson, the engineer, recalled: 'The line will consist of 7¼ miles . . . through open, sparsely inhabited country composed of elm-lined lanes and hayfields under which is the heavy London clay. Except for an arable field at Uxbridge, it is all meadow land throughout, mainly devoted to heavy crops of hay for the London market.'

In 1924-5, the flat junction was replaced by a 1200-foot-long 'fly-under' to avoid Uxbridge branch trains conflicting with the main line. The retaining walls used 12,000 tons of concrete and bricks.

No. 68, one of the 'C' class loco-motives built by Neilson & Co. in 1891. They were of a similar kind to a batch built at the same time for Sir Edward Watkin's South Eastern Railway. The four Metro-politan locos were a modification of James Stirling's original design.

One of the class, No. 67, disgraced herself on one of her first trips by coming to a halt near Marlborough Road and being run into by the next train. Seventeen passengers were injured. No. 68 was broken up in 1919.

The 'navigators' (navvies) dug the canals and then the railways of nineteenth-century Britain. They were men who earned a name for lawlessness, drunkenness and poor morals. But this was, perhaps, a biased view. The Harrow & Uxbridge Railway contract and the nearby GWR and GCR works saw the end of the railway 'navvy'.

This man – probably either Norfolk Joe or Busy Dave Simmons, two of the men in charge of the bricklayers who built the Roxeth viaduct – is seen outside his traditional turf hut near Rayners Lane. Note his dress, including leather straps round his legs, the open fireplace, and the clothes drying on the bushes to the right.

The Roxeth viaduct between Rayners Lane junction and Roxeth (named South Harrow by the District Railway) is ¾ mile long. In this 1903 picture, Bott & Stennett's locomotive 'Gordon' has brought a train of wagons along the temporary track laid over the fields. The bricklayers are at work by the hoists. If you examine the picture closely, you can see a man standing rather dangerously on the buffers between the locomotive and the trucks, while two other men talk between the third and fourth vehicles. The viaduct was called 'a fine specimen of engineering skill' when it was completed in 1904. A siding was opened to Roxeth Gas Works on 4 October 1910, but the Metropolitan never worked passenger trains to South Harrow. The District service began on 1 March 1910.

Rayners Lane in 1903 was truly a junction in the middle of nowhere. The bridge carrying the ancient lane to Pinner is nearing completion, and temporary track can be seen curving towards Harrow (left) and the viaduct (right), with a section of light railway in the foreground.

A year has passed and the junction is almost ready for opening. One of Bott & Stennett's wagons stands on the Harrow track (left). The contractor's saw mills can be seen to the right. Timber from trees cut down during the building of the line were used for fence poles. The signal box was demolished by a runaway train in the mid-1930s. When the halt opened on 26 May 1906 it quickly became a byword for bleakness in winter. Drivers and passengers complained that the fire was always out, and the place was known as 'Pneumonia Junction'.

Ruislip Manor bridge under construction in 1902-3, with horse power being used. Later the track was to become Victoria Road. The station opened on 5 August 1912.

Ruislip station under construction in February 1903 when some of the Met's top management were paying a visit. In the foreground is a section of light railway track and the tank used for watering the contractor's locomotives.

Not long after this picture was taken part of the brickwork of the station's main gable collapsed while under construction, and the three men working on it were injured. They were E. Weatherley, member of a well-known Ruislip family of builders, Bertie Lacy and Frank Payne. Payne broke his leg and had to be taken to Uxbridge Hospital.

By the autumn of 1903 Ruislip station was almost ready, but the running lines still had to be laid. If you look to the right of the station, you can see one of Bott & Stennett's wagons on a section of track in what is now the station yard. The footbridge was moved nearer the station canopy in 1928.

The new station at Ruislip will soon open, though the glaziers' marks remain on the windows. The local paper sent along a reporter who recorded: 'No doubt the station is built for the future accommodation of the most picturesque residential neighbourhood near London, where many building sites are already in the making. Ruislip, it may be mentioned, will be the only station building between Uxbridge and Harrow.'

One of the earliest suburban developments at Ruislip was just to the west of High Street on the Park House estate. This view of 1876 shows the house (which still stands) and its then extensive grounds, 'a capital country house with stabling, outbuildings, a lodge, ornamental pond and a forcinghouse, with furnace.'

RUISLIP PARK.

Making the approach slopes at Long Lane bridge, Ickenham, by the site of the future Hillingdon station. Steamrollers can be seen flattening the surface. The construction and maintenance of the slopes at each bridge along the line gave much trouble in the early days because of the nature of London clay. Brushwood and bark from local trees were used to provide foundations for the ballast and hardcore. The trees in the background are on the Swakeleys Estate, which was developed from 1922.

Park Road bridge, Uxbridge, was the largest bridge on the Harrow and Uxbridge branch. A temporary wooden road bridge was erected to carry Park Road, with a massive box structure of iron for the main sewer. The trees on the right are in the small country estate of Coaxden, part of which had to be bought for the railway cutting to be built.

Colonel Cox of Harefield Place, Ickenham was one of the main landowners in the area. He willingly sold his land for the line. Cox (1835-1913) was a member of the well known banking company and he saw that the new railway would bring prosperity to Uxbridge. He allowed the contractors free use of his land to run a light railway from the Grand Union canal at Frays Wharf up the hill – by means of back shunts – to Uxbridge Common and down to the line at Hillingdon, for the purpose of bringing building supplies and gravel.

He was one of those present at the great opening day feast in a marquee decorated with Icelandic poppies outside Uxbridge station on 30 June 1904, where he made a speech. The vast meal included such delights as salmon, lobster salad, ris de veau à la crème, kidneys à la campagne, turkey, roast chicken, York ham, galantine of veal, ox tongue, pigeon pies, sirloin of beef, roast lamb, chartreuse jelly, pine creams, meringues and compôte of fruit – all washed down with bottle after bottle of best hock, claret and champagne.

Uxbridge Gazette.
SPECIAL EDITION.
Opening of Uxbridge-Harrow Railway.

Thursday, June 30th, 1904.   One Penny.

FREDERICK COX, Esq.,
Local Director of the Uxbridge-Harrow Railway.

When the new line was finished the Metropolitan purchased from one of the contractors this curious loco-motive. 'Nellie' puffed up and down Neasden yards for many years and was the only locomotive permitted to cross one of the weaker bridges over the river Brent at the power station.

This picture of one of the early type of electric trains with mem-bers of the Press near Rayners Lane has been seen before. But recently some more facts have emerged about the day. The gentle-man with the silk topper standing on the track (centre) is Lord Aberconway, Chairman of the Metropolitan. Before the trip the Press and other guests were enter-tained to lunch at the Great Central Hotel. One reporter from Uxbridge has left us this record, complete with McGonigal-style verses:

'The train started from Baker Street without the jerk normally associated with the old steam trains.

It was not a pleasant fancy,
Nor a vision of the night
Which changed, as by some magic spell,
The darkness into light.
Shades of Watt, of Armstrong, Rennie,
Shades of Stephenson, Brunel,
Shedding gleams so clear and mellow
Where but darkness reigned before.
Bidding fumes all black and stifling
To depart for evermore.

Let your inspiration aid me
In my efforts here, to tell

Of the wonders of that journey –
Of that gliding, smooth and swift,
As if Jove, the god of lighting,
Had bestowed some superior gift.

What a mighty demonstration
Of the progress of the age!
Can be found no brighter page
An experience to remember
Was that really pleasant run,
With its journey well nigh over
Ere we felt it scarce begun!'

During the 1880s and 1890s the Metropolitan Railway continued to push outwards from London into the Chilterns. Pinner was reached in 1885, Rickmansworth two years later, and the first train from Chesham ran on 8 July 1889. Chesham town elders were, like most other official bodies of that time, anxious to welcome the new age of steam. This was the scene on that great day, as the town dignitaries pack into the official train, hauled by 'Wellington', while less fortunate townsfolk watch in the sun from the neighbouring bank. The coaches are the original Metropolitan 'straight door' stock, dating from the 1860s. Note the large figures '2' on the centre panel of the doors – a popular joke of the day was that of an ignorant traveller who had been challenged by a Met inspector for journeying in a higher class than that indicated on his ticket. He is supposed to have replied: 'I paid twopence for my ticket so naturally I got into a carriage with a "2" marked on it.' The second class disappeared with electrification.

METROPOLITAN RAILWAY

—:o:—

Inspection of the

CHESHAM EXTENSION,

WEDNESDAY, MAY 15th, 1889.

• MENU •

Clear Mock Turtle.

Mayonnaise of Salmon.   Lobsters in Shell.

Dressed Crabs.

Fore-Quarters of Lamb.

Roast Surrey Capons.   York Ham.

Ox Tongues.

Pigeon Pies.   Sirloin of Beef.   Pressed Beef.

Galantine of Chicken.

Wine Jellies.   Maraschino Jellies.

Blancmangers.   Maids of Honor.   French Pastry.

Neapolitan Ices.

Cheese.   Watercress.

DESSERT AND COFFEE.

Sherry.   Claret.

Champagne : } Perinet et Fils.
            } Moet et Chandon, Brut Imperial.

Spiers and Pond, Limited,
Refreshment Contractors.

Some idea of the importance attached to the opening of the Metropolitan Railway by the small towns of the Chilterns can be gauged by this menu card for the great celebratory dinner to mark the inspection of the extension to Chesham in May 1889. Amid the splendour of the lobsters and champagne was one significant delicacy – watercress. This was widely grown locally, and Metropolitan trains made special collections for the London markets.

5
Great-Grandfather's Day
1904 to 1933
The Metropolitan Railway's
halcyon days

The new Selbie House, Baker Street, home of the Metropolitan Railway and now, of course, part of the Baker Street London Transport complex. The building dates from 1912, and is interesting for the use of glazed brick. It was designed to reflect the pride of the railway in its new (electric) image. It has been suggested that the frieze of railway symbols may be actual material from the old company rolling stock and track.

Old Finchley Road station was a dismal place. Here the long series of tunnels came to an end and the journey to Metro-land began. When the station was rebuilt for the Bakerloo extension in the late 1930s, London Transport engineers faced one of their most difficult tasks when they had to underpin the buildings.

By GWR to Liverpool Street. A rare picture of a Metropolitan electric locomotive standing at the old Bishop's Road station, Paddington, before the First World War. The locomotive is waiting to haul a GWR suburban train through the tunnels via Edgware Road and Baker Street to the City. The service originally ran to Aldgate, but in later days the siding at Liverpool Street Metropolitan was the terminus for these rush hour services, which ceased on 16 September 1939.

From 1907 the trains were electrically hauled, first by the camelback type of locomotives, then the Metropolitan Vickers class. Early in the morning, no fewer than four electric locomotives coupled together would run up from Neasden to Baker Street. One would be detached to proceed to Liverpool Street, the other three reversing on to the 'inner' rail of the Circle Line, and proceeding to Paddington to start the day's operations.

Old King's Cross station in 1910. In this changeover period the new Metropolitan train is working on electrified lines.

Note the vast higgledy-piggledy array of enamelled iron advertisements that were a feature of all the London Underground stations of the time. Many long-established advertisers, including Pear's soap, Emu boot polish and Bovril can be seen. Station names were so dwarfed that it was small wonder the passengers missed stations if they were unfamiliar with the steamy stop. This station, with its massive roof span of 90 feet, was built as early as 1862.

High Road, Brondesbury

This was Kilburn High Road, near the Metropolitan station, in about 1908, a contrast indeed to the busy main road of today! Kilburn was one of the earliest metropolitan suburbs and one could rent a respectable red-brick villa for £70 a year – and open an account at one of the shops on the right.

The locomotive siding at Harrow in about 1908, with two of the camel-back locomotives waiting to take trains of steam stock back to London. The steam engine here is one of the 'E' type. The locomotive changeover was at Wembley Park from 1 November 1906, and this point was used even after the Harrow station rebuilding of 1908. Both places were superseded in 1925, with the electrification being completed through to Rickmansworth.

Another 'E' class 4-4-0 tank works bunker forward as it leaves Neasden with a six-coach bogie set of 'Ashbury' stock. The locomotive, No. 77, survived to pass into the possession of the London Passenger Transport Board in 1933, as L46. This locomotive was built at Neasden.

One of the electric locomotives purchased to deal with the main line traffic in 1907, this new engine heads north with a train of assorted passenger stock in 1910. The locomotives were built by British Thomson Houston, and with the earlier camel-back Westinghouse electric locomotives formed the original electric fleet. A considerable amount of land was acquired at Stoke Mandeville on which it was proposed to build a new Works Depot; Neasden Depot was to be transferred to the Great Central Railway.

Willesden Green's first station, a cottage-style building of 1879. On the left a tram of the Metropolitan Electric Tramways rattles towards Willesden Green, bringing visitors from rural Finchley to town. Men and horses stand, without major traffic worries, in the centre of the road. A poster advertises 'Late Theatre trains' on the newly electrified railway.

Collision: not one of the better days for the shunters at Willesden Green sidings at the turn of the century! This Beyer Peacock locomotive 18 (*Hercules*) had her dents ironed out, and served until 1926.

Locomotive 77, a 0-4-4 tank, complete with a full load of coal and carrying Aylesbury destination boards, as though ready to head a northbound train. This picture is believed to date from the turn of the century. The 'E' class, of which this is an example, were built between 1896 and 1901 for duties on the Extension Line. It passed into London Transport stock as L46. The last of the class (except L44, preserved at Quainton Road) was scrapped as late as 1962.

The old enclosed roof of the original King's Cross Metropolitan station was removed, and the station seen here in 1913. On the right are the Widened Lines which allowed steam trains of the Midland and the Great Northern Railways to reach Moorgate. At one period these tracks were electrified for the use of Met trains between King's Cross and the City. The present King's Cross station further west was opened in 1941.

Inside Neasden Power Station in 1906. A line of Babcock & Wilcox boilers, fitted with superheaters and chain grate stokers, stand in a formidable array to supply the smart new electric services. The *Railway Magazine* of September 1903 reported that a power station was also proposed at Park Royal for the GWR, to work the Hammersmith to Bishop's Road section.

This photograph, taken on 25 February 1915, shows steel girder sections being swung into position during the construction of the Kilburn, Shootup Hill bridge, ready for the additional tracks.

Bridge rebuilding: snow outlines the timbers in use for the work on the North London Railway crossing bridge near West Hampstead in 1915.

Canons Park Station, on the 1932 Metropolitan extension to Stanmore. The district offered a wide range of places to live, even as early as 1934. You could soon be living in a smart semi-detached house with metal windows, every modern aid in the kitchen and even a garage for 15 shillings (75p) a week.

One of the camel-back (British Westinghouse) locomotives (No. 6), seen here at Vine Street goods depot, Farringdon, in about 1909. This small depot opened on 1 September of that year and consisted of only two sidings. Freight traffic was worked from Finchley Road goods depot and was restricted to fourteen wagons, usually electrically hauled. The depot closed on 30 June 1936.

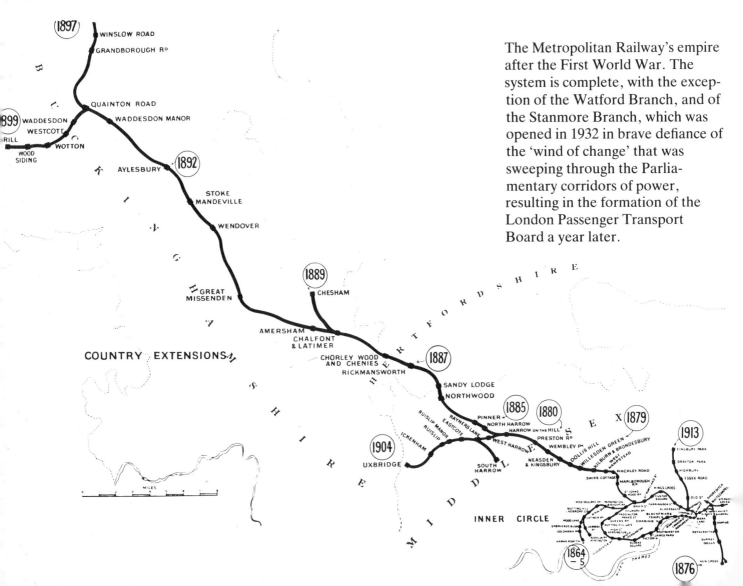

The Metropolitan Railway's empire after the First World War. The system is complete, with the exception of the Watford Branch, and of the Stanmore Branch, which was opened in 1932 in brave defiance of the 'wind of change' that was sweeping through the Parliamentary corridors of power, resulting in the formation of the London Passenger Transport Board a year later.

COUNTRY EXTENSIONS

INNER CIRCLE

The first multiple-unit electric service ran from January 1905 between Baker Street and Uxbridge. (The newly opened Uxbridge branch had been worked for six months at first by steam.) Electrification of the main Extension Line was not extended northwards from Harrow until after the First World War. From 1906 all Chesham, Verney Junction and Aylesbury trains were hauled clear of the London tunnels up to Wembley Park by electric loco-motives; from 19 July 1908 Harrow became the principal locomotive changeover point, and the station itself was enlarged.

This photograph shows the coal-ing stage at Harrow on 9 October ber 1920, with the Metro-Cammell electric locomotive 15 running light to pick up a London-bound train.

Locomotive 78 coaling up at the Harrow coaling stage on the same day. The coal baskets carried about one hundredweight of loco coal; during steam days they were positioned also at the ends of selected inner London stations. The coal wagon, which has just been unloaded, has been brought up from the Midlands via Quainton Road. Locomotive 78 was a Neasden-built class 'E' 0-4-4 tank, which had been built in the late 1890s; it did not survive into London Transport days. Inci-dentally, behind the stage are some early Metro-land houses.

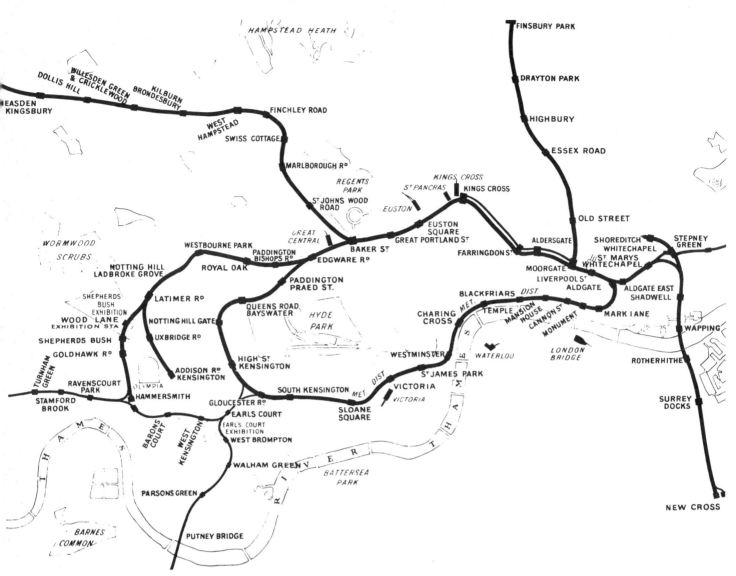

The Metropolitan's urban network
in 1919, the essential system that
passed to the LPTB in 1933.

Some idea of the still rural nature
of the area around Preston Road in
the early 1930s can be glimpsed
from this view, taken from the last
Metro-land guide.
Here, just beyond the hedge-lined
lane, the first new houses are
already mingling with the occasional farm cottage.

SMALL SECTION OF PAVILION TEA ROOMS

EASTCOTE, MIDDLESEX.

The Pavilion, Field End Road, Eastcote, was the largest and most famous of the old Metro-Land pleasure gardens. The grounds covered 32 acres and up to 4000 people could be accommodated under cover if it rained.
For many London children, it was their first introduction to the countryside.

This bill cancels all previous issues and comes operation on July 15th.

Metropolitan and Great Central Railways.

BUCKINGHAM MARKET.

MARKET TICKETS, THIRD CLASS,

ARE NOW ISSUED ON

SATURDAYS

FROM

AYLESBURY TO BUCKINGHAM

Return 1/11 Fare,

AVAILABLE ONLY BY FOLLOWING TRAINS:—

		A.M.	A.M.	A.M.
AYLESBURY	...dep.	7 30	9 47	11 45
BUCKINGHAM	...arr.	8 52	11 4	P.M. 2 12

RETURNING ON DAY OF ISSUE ONLY.

		P.M.		P.M.
BUCKINGHAM	...dep.	3 8		5 43
AYLESBURY	...arr.	4 2		6 37

UXBRIDGE MARKET.

MARKET TICKETS, THIRD CLASS,

ARE NOW ISSUED

TO UXBRIDGE ON SATURDAYS

From HARROW,	Return Fare	8d.	Third Class.
,, WEST HARROW	,,	7d.	,, ,,
,, ICKENHAM	,,	3d.	,, ,,

Available by any Train after 12-0 noon, and for Return by any Train same day.

Passengers holding Market Tickets travelling without personal luggage, may carry with them 60 lbs. of Marketing Goods at Owner's Risk, free of charge.

Market Tickets are not transferable, and should they be used by any other Train, or on any other day than as specified, or to or from any other Stations than those named upon them, the Tickets will be cancelled and the full ordinary fares charged.

Children under Three Years of age, Free; Three and under Twelve, Half-fares.

All Bills of a previous date are hereby cancelled.

Tickets and Bills can be obtained at the Stations.

BY ORDER.

8 5027   STAFFORD & CO., LTD., PRINTERS, NETHERFIELD, NOTTS.   3,000

Market tickets were available on certain trains to markets as far away as Buckingham, as this hand-bill shows. It was understood that passengers using these tickets would travel homewards with plenty of materials and food, and the ticket allowed each person to carry 60 lb weight of purchases.

The Buckingham Market was reached by Metropolitan train to Verney Junction, and then by L&NW railway to Buckingham. The Aylesbury & Buckingham Railway had been opened as long ago as 1868, within five years or so of the first underground steam trains in London.

Interiors of the new compartment trains offered some of the most comfortable seats on any London suburban service. 'The new rolling stock is beautifully designed; elegant upholstery and fittings, refined and comfortable,' said a press report in 1927.

A rare picture of the original East-cote halt of 26 May 1906, and one of the 1905 stock trains. The fields in the background were developed in the 1930s by T.F. Nash and Rotherham Estates. The halt here has oil lamps and the name board would have had white letters on a red background.

Eastcote cheap tickets: A typical range of fares for Londoners to take a Whit Sunday outing to the delights of the Uxbridge Line stations.

CHEAP TICKETS WILL BE ISSUED

FROM

LONDON STATIONS (Met. Rly.)

TO

Rayners Lane, Eastcote, Ruislip Manor, Ruislip, Ickenham and Uxbridge,

AS UNDER :—

FROM	RETURN FARES, THIRD CLASS.			
	To Rayners Lane.	To Eastcote.	To Ruislip Manor, Ruislip and Ickenham.	To Uxbridge
NEW CROSS (L.B. & S.C.)	1 4	1 5	1/6	1 9
Surrey Docks	1 3	1 4	1 5	1 7
Rotherhithe				
Wapping	1 2	1 3	1,4	1 6
Shadwell				
St. Mary's (Whitechapel	1,1	1,2	1 3	1 5
Aldgate East				
Cannon Street				
Monument	1 1	1 1	1 3	1 5
Mark Lane				
Aldgate				
Liverpool Street				
Finsbury Park	1/3	1,3	1/5	1 7
Drayton Park				
Highbury				
Essex Road	1/2	1 2	1 4	1/6
Old Street				
Moorgate Street	1 1	1 1	1 3	1 5
Aldersgate				
Farringdon Street	1 1	1 1	1 2	1 5
King's Cross	1 1	1 1	1 1	1 4
Euston Square	1/-	1/-	1 1	1 3
Portland Road			1	
BAKER STREET				
St. John's Wood Road	11d.	11d.	11d.	1 3
Marlboro' Road				
Swiss Cottage	11d.	11d.	11d.	1 2
Finchley Road				
West Hampstead	10d.	11d.	11d.	1 2
Kilburn-Brondesbury	10d.	11d.	11d.	1 2
Willesden Green	10d.	10d.	10d.	1 2
Edgware Road	11d.	11d.	11d.	1/3
Paddington Praed Street	11d.	11d.	11d.	1 3
" " Bishop's Road				
Bayswater				
Notting Hill Gate				
High Street, Kensington	11d.	1 -	1 1	1 3
Gloucester Road				
South Kensington				

Change at Moorgate St.

Available for Return by any Train on day of issue only.

TICKETS WILL BE ISSUED AS UNDER :—

To Rayners Lane
Eastcote
Ruislip Manor   By all Trains from Baker Street up to 5.30 p.m. on
Ruislip   BANK HOLIDAY MONDAY.
Ickenham
Uxbridge

THROUGH TICKETS AT CHEAP FARES WILL ALSO BE ISSUED FROM STATIONS ON THE BAKERLOO LINE (VIA BAKER STREET) TO ALL STATIONS.

CHEAP EXCURSION TICKETS WILL ALSO BE ISSUED TO PINNER, NORTHWOOD, RICKMANSWORTH, CHORLEY WOOD, CHALFONT ROAD, CHESHAM, AMERSHAM, GREAT MISSENDEN, WENDOVER, AYLESBURY, ETC.

For particulars see programme obtainable at all Stations.

For Times of Trains please see other side.

The First World War arrived on the Bank Holiday in early August when Londoners traditionally set out to enjoy themselves. This 1914 handbill, with its list of excursion stations on the Uxbridge branch, gives an idea of railway costs before the First World War. Some of the stations have, of course, now disappeared; others have been renamed.

Occasionally there could be infuriating delays for waiting Metro-land residents when their train failed to arrive for the morning journey to town. In this unpublished picture the gang is attempting to lift, with the aid of jacks placed under the end chassis frame, this 'MV' car which left the road while being prepared for the morning service. Some of these cars were built for steam service but were converted for running with 'MV' cars in 1927.

Train of gate-ended stock in the very early days of electric operation on the line to Uxbridge. The train has stopped for the photographer by the site of Ickenham Halt, which opened on 25 September 1905.

'The cars, which are of two classes, are 52½ft long' said an official Metropolitan press release. 'At both ends of each car is a closed-in vestibule . . . and access to this from the station platform is given by means of a patent device which, when operated by the conductor, moves into the frame of the car.'

The second class seats in non-smoking sections were upholstered in 'Art Green' moquette, while smoking saloons had green leather. Third class travellers had buffalo hide seats.

It was the efforts of two Ickenham parish councillors, David Brikett and Harry Weedon, that obtained a 'halt' for Ickenham. The French spelling was used in early timetables, but never on the station signs.

North Harrow in 1927, with the old station buildings on the right, not long before rebuilding, and the Headstone Hotel through the bridge. A board advertises E.S. Reid's new houses shortly to be erected at Rayners Lane, although there is no roadway as yet, just a cart track.

This young lady is cycling through the peaceful centre of Ruislip in about 1910. She may have lived in one of the new houses then being built on the Park House estate. On the left is the boundary of the old mansion. A little further along is the Swan Inn (Salter's Fine Ales. Teas and accommodation. H. Ryder. Prop.).

An early issue of *Metro-land* says: 'Ruislip, in common with that beautiful part of Middlesex in which it lies, makes two appeals to the Londoner. One is expressed in its charm as a holiday resort; the other as a place of residence.

'When there are new homes available in a countryside so near, so healthy and historic as Ruislip, many Londoners will be glad to quit their musty residences for a rural homestead.

Ruislip Sports Day, 1908. All the village has turned out, as well as crowds of visitors who have come by Metropolitan Railway, to see the procession to the field near Manor Farm. On the left is Mrs Riddle's newspaper and sweet shop, a social centre of village life for many years. The Uxbridge Registrar attended here once a week until the late 1930s.

The annual sports days continued until 1914.

Third class saloon coach, for the joint service with the Great Western Railway on the Hammersmith & City branch.

The first 'Dreadnought' coach, with nine compartments, as delivered to the railway by Metro-Cammell for the Extension Line services.

Lord Aberconway, an 0-6-4 tank seen here with Metro-Vickers camel-back electric locomotive No. 2 near Neasden, was built in 1915. This locomotive was trans-ferred to LNER ownership as No. 6154 with the demise of the Met, with its sisters – *Robert H. Selbie, Charles Jones* and *Brill*.

These class G locomotives were the first named steam engines since the very earliest days of the company, though a locomotive of the Wotton Tramway had borne the name *Brill* in earlier times.

Hartwell church peeps across the water in the foreground – this is a typical 'Metro-land' promotional illustration of the 1920s. Here all appears to be sylvan peace, although on a normal ramblers' outing the insect inhabitants had to be reckoned with – mosquitoes, wasps and other pests all attracted by the hot, happy children and their jam sandwiches.

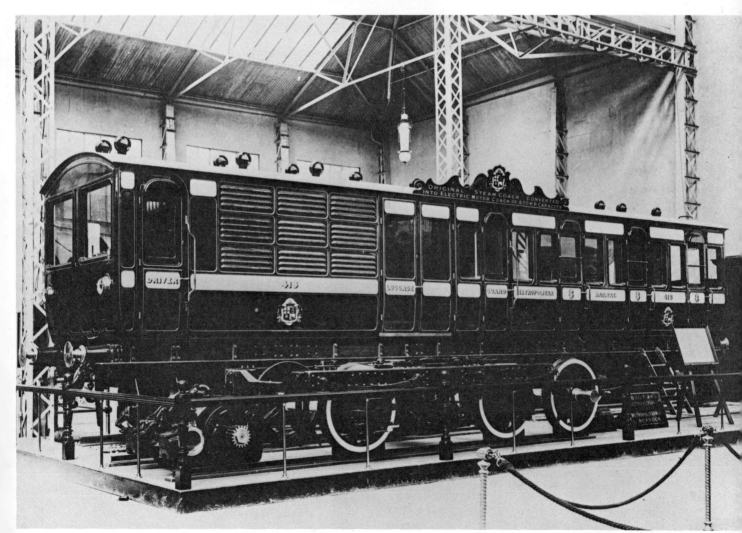

The British Empire Exhibition was held at Wembley in 1924 and 1925; in both years the Metropolitan had a display stand in the Palace of Engineering. In 1924 this 'bogie' stock car was displayed. The ornate sign along the roof edge of the carriage reads: 'Original steam coach converted into electric motor car of 600 HP capacity.' In the foreground is one of the motor bogies, and another sign reading: 'Built and electrically equipped at the Metropolitan Works, Neasden.' Trains of this type worked on the Uxbridge and later on the Stanmore line. In the late 1930s London Transport carried out some strange experiments by painting some of the trains red, green and grey. Fortunately, good taste prevailed, and varnished teak livery was reinstated.

The Metropolitan breakdown train, under the charge of the handsome 2-6-4 tank No. 114 of the 'K' class. As LNER 6160 it survived until the 1946 renumbering scheme, when it was reallocated the number 9071. At that time it was one of only two survivors of this class, which had been designed for high-speed passenger and freight working up to Verney Junction.

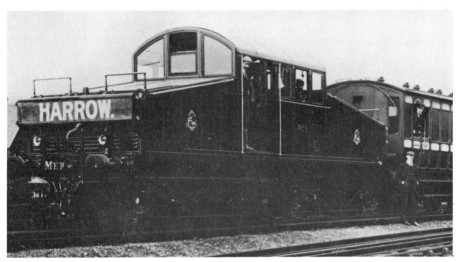

One of the Westinghouse electric locomotives introduced in 1905 for hauling steam stock trains from Baker Street to Wembley Park, where steam locomotives took over for the long journey to the Chilterns. There were ten of these rather ungainly machines. The ugly destination blinds were replaced by standard enamel plates in about 1911. The train here is made up of a set of 'bogie' type carriages, which were later converted for multiple electric operation.

The remains of a motor car and a trailer vehicle outside Neasden works in 1907 following the serious accident of 26 October. The disaster happened in thick fog at West Hampstead when two Uxbridge trains collided and three passengers were killed. Later, car 46 was rebuilt as a gauging vehicle and used for measuring the main line for Pullman cars. The car was then used, with parts from another similar car, to build a shuttle car used on the Uxbridge and later Rickmansworth–Watford and Wembley Park to Stanmore services.

A Monday accident at Moorgate Street in the 1920s. This Harrow train crashed into the buffers and some passengers were severely shaken. This view shows the extent of the impact damage to the train. Workmen are seen trying to cut the remains of the impacted wood-work free from the frame of the train.

The Met's 'top brass' are inspecting the damage, which has been hidden from the public gaze by hastily erected Metropolitan goods tarpaulins.

Metropolitan goods services were important, and fleets of carts and motor lorries provided a swift service. Here Thorneycroft vehicles leave Baker Street station in 1928.

'Darling, will meet you for tea in Chiltern Court after your shopping trip – it's so *chic*!' A romantic sketch of Chiltern Court in the 1920s, an oasis for early Metro-land residents awaiting their Pullman train into the Chilterns. The restaurant closed in recent times.

A Metro-Vickers electric locomotive, with special cut out section
to show the driving units, being
placed in position for the 1925
exhibition.

This was No. 15, with interior
painted white so visitors could see
'the works'. Under the 1927
naming scheme No. 5 was titled
Wembley 1924, its plaques sur-
mounted by the Wembley lion. It
was withdrawn after a collision in
Neasden yards on 18 September
1951.

One of the 'F' class locomotives,
built by the Yorkshire Engine Co.
in 1901, near Northwick Park in
the early 1920s. The locomotive
lasted in service until 1962.

Off to Chesham. This is No. 14 (*Benjamin Disraeli*) heading the Chesham Pullman train passing at speed through Wembley Park in 1923. The twenty Met–Vickers locomotives were named with associations of the City and the Chiltern Hills following a meeting of the Metropolitan's Traffic Committee of 18 March 1927. No. 14 continued in service until 7 March 1962.

The end of an eventful career. Neasden Yard, in 1925, was used to collect most of the remaining 4-4-0 tanks of the 'A' and 'B' classes, many of which had become surplus to the Met's needs when it took delivery of new 2-6-4 tanks after the First World War. One of these locomotives, No. 7, was sold to the Mersey Railway in Liverpool for departmental duties. As Mersey No. 2, this stalwart old locomotive survived until 1939. It was one of the first batch of engines purchased in the 1860s, and once carried the name *Orion*.

This photograph was taken at Birkenhead Central on 15 September 1930.

Outside Belmont Road goods yard, Uxbridge, c. 1905. Although the company's name appeared on the local delivery carts, they were in fact operated by a contractor.

An important part of Metropolitan operations was goods traffic. This is a rare shot showing inside the goods warehouse at Uxbridge, with a handworked crane loading trucks with flour from one of the many local mills.

'Eastcote is one of those picturesque rural villages that popularity has failed to spoil, and its straggling main street, formed of old-fashioned cottages and farm houses, maintains a peaceful charm in spite of its nearness to the metropolis . . . on all sides there are plenty of fields, intersected with many footpaths' (*Metro-land*).

This scene was near Eastcote House – and amazingly, it is still much the same today.

Hillingdon station approach from the south in the late 1920s, long before the A40 was built. The station opened on 10 December 1923 to serve the Metropolitan's Hillingdon Mount Estate on one side, and the Swakeleys Estate, then being developed by Stedman & Clark, on the other. Surprisingly, the huts still exist on the left-hand side, but the road was widened in 1938, sweeping away the buildings on the right.

Rayners Lane in 1929, looking towards Pinner and North Harrow. In August of that year the first sods were dug for the Harrow Garden Village Estate, the Metropolitan Country Estates' first venture into lower-priced, well-designed housing. In this view you can see the stakes in the field marking the site of the new Imperial Drive to North Harrow. The booking hut is typical of those at Met halts in this period.

It's holiday time for these London children arriving at Eastcote in 1932. A similar picture was used in our companion volume, *Metro Memories*; but this shot was taken later and shows one of the 'T' stock trains in the background and the canopy over the 'up' platform, a facility added to shield large parties from inclement summer weather while they waited for the special trains to take them home. The special stock would be 'stabled' in sidings along the line at Ruislip during the day.

Highfields, Hillingdon was frequently advertised in 'Metro-Land' magazine. The nearby Metropolitan Country Estate's Hillingdon Mount Estate was 'only 15 miles from London in a delightfully rural district. The estate adjoins Hillingdon station on the Metropolitan Railway and is within easy reach of the picturesque old market town of Uxbridge.

Harrow-on-the-Hill was a steam/electric changeover point until 1925. One of the then new 'H' class locomotives (designed by Charles Jones and built by Kerr, Stuart & Co., 1920-1) arrives with a train from Aylesbury.

The Northwick Park Estate at Harrow (the other one is near Moreton-in-Marsh, Gloucestershire) was sold for building just before the First World War. But although some roadways were constructed, the houses did not arrive until the early 1920's. The station was opened in 1923.

The opposition. The Chilterns attracted parties on packaged coach tours as well as railway travellers in the 1920s. The vehicles were called charabancs, a word that has now disappeared completely but was in constant use then to describe the convertible type of coach, which has stepped seating to enhance the view. It was, of course, wonderful on a balmy day in the hills, but watch out if there was a sudden downpour! This party, which seemed to have consisted almost entirely of men with the *de rigueur* trilby, is climbing out of High Wycombe in 1924 on the way to Amersham.

In the first reference to country walking in *Metro-land*, the reader was urged to visit the area of the Misbourne Valley, still the heart of 'London Country' Chilterns. Milton's Cottage was a favourite objective for the hiker arriving by Met. In nearby Coleshill, the once famous old oak under which, it was said, the poet Edmund Waller penned his muse, also attracted the railway traveller in Edwardian days; as this illustration shows, it was fashionable to have your photograph taken inside the open bole of the tree.

Waller was a cousin of John Hampden, the opponent of King Charles I. Waller was MP for Amersham and was regarded as one of the greatest poets of his time, perhaps because he praised Cromwell in one verse and later penned lines in praise of Charles II. He was born at Stock Place, Coleshill, on the heights above the Misbourne Valley, in 1605.

Another interest for the earliest travellers on the new Extension Line was noting the country crafts of hedging, thatching and straw plaiting. Here another Buckinghamshire craft, lace-making, is being undertaken by a patient, quick-fingered plaiter outside her cottage. Much of the old craft was lost with the change of fashions and mass manufacture from abroad after the First World War.

Late Edwardian England was a very patriotic place. At village summer carnivals all over the Chilterns decorated floats such as this, with Union Jacks everywhere – from the top of the cart to the head of the horse – could be seen. The girls, if more coy and overdressed than those on carnival floats today, at least had the same desire: to enjoy the occasion. This float, from a Hertfordshire village near Berkhamsted, was celebrating a local event, at about the time of the first Metropolitan Railway electrification.

It's a summer day in Rickmansworth (3 July 1930, to be precise) and this brand new AEC Regal bus is on the St Albans via Watford route of the Lewis Omnibus Company of Market Street, Watford. 'Pleasure seekers and others will find the services provided by the Lewis Omnibus Company a particularly convenient means of reaching the Chilterns' said an advertisement in *Metro-land*. Lewis routes included Rickmansworth to the Chalfonts, Berkhamsted and south to Slough and Windsor. The company also took over the Met's feeder bus service from Watford Met station into the town centre.

Chesham station in 1926.

A turn-of-the-century view of Chesham, taken about 1904 from the footpath that climbs the hill beside the station. Many of the station features, including the coal yard, remained without major alterations until recent times.

Examples of metal season tickets, made of silver (hallmarked) and enamel. The left-hand one is the reverse of a second class season (the round area is believed to have contained the validity of the ticket). The other is a round first class ticket. They date from around 1919, and both bear the marks of Mr Selbie, the general manager. They were designed to be hung from men's watch chains (the days before women's lib, of course!)

By 1933 houses were rapidly spreading over the fields between Rayners Lane and North Harrow. This is a typical advertisement of that time. The prices make interesting comparison with those of today.

WATFORD'S NEW RAILWAY

WATFORD and Croxley Green have now at their door a new railway which means much to local convenience and prosperity. It has been jointly constructed by the Metropolitan and the London and North Eastern Railway Companies and provides an alternative route to London; a new way to the North, and an active stimulant to local development.

The new route affords Watford and Croxley Green the easiest and most direct means of access to all parts of London; it brings the towns of Uxbridge, Chesham and Aylesbury within easy reach; it provides direct means of communication with a large number of important places in the Midlands, North of England and Scotland, and, by means of escalator and lift connections at Baker Street and Marylebone Stations, links up with the whole of London's Tube system.

Fast and frequent electric trains are run to and from Baker Street, and well-appointed steam trains are operated to and from Marylebone, whilst "Through" Electric City trains are provided both morning and evening. Quarterly, Monthly and

seven-day Season Tickets are issued together with special fares for Workmen. Cheap fare facilities are in operation for Excursion parties.

To those who work in Croxley Green or Watford the new route makes possible residence in the popular countryside served by the Metropolitan and Great Central Joint Railway known as "Metroland" and, at the same time, gives the pleasure-seeker a wider range of charming beauty spots to explore.

The new line is protected throughout its length by the latest type of automatic signalling, and in the construction of the line and stations everything conducive to the comfort and convenience of the travelling public has been carefully considered.

A few examples of Season Ticket Rates together with particulars of the first and last trains are shown on the back of this folder, and the Commercial Manager, Baker Street Station, N.W.1, and Passenger Manager, Liverpool Street Station, E.C.2, will be glad, on application, to give further information on any subject affecting the new line.

TRAVEL BY THE NEW ROUTE — EASIEST AND BEST!

Watford's new railway. The crowds depicted in this unusual proof copy of the company's joint promotion with the London & North Eastern Railway in 1925 hardly materialized. The station remained bedded completely in housing estates, and remained quite a distance from the shopping centre of Watford, where it was hoped to construct the terminus of the Watford extension.

New trains for Watford were introduced in 1927. This is one of the first batch, built by Metropolitan Vickers. Note the buffers and chain couplings. The next two batches (the 'MW' stock) had the later standard electric train buckeye couplings and no buffers. Steam 'Dreadnought' stock, was often marshalled with the electric motor cars in the early days of the Watford services. The trains also appeared on Uxbridge Line duties. In London Transport days the whole group of trains of this type were classified 'T' stock. They last ran in 1962.

This amateur photographer's snap of 4-4-4 T No. 103 shows the locomotive, with three men cramped on the footplate, as it waits to head north with an Aylesbury-bound train in 1932.

The Metropolitan Railway carried as much as 162,764 tons of coal, 2,478,212 tons of minerals and 1,015,501 tons of other goods during its last year of independent operation (1932). The company owned 544 goods vehicles. This is a view of a typical goods train headed by an 'H' class locomotive between Wendover and Great Missenden in the early 1930s. The locomotive carries a disc numbered 3.

Ruislip village, in the days before
Metro-land. This 1905 snap of
Ruislip village centre shows the
village less than eighty years ago; a
place unpeopled and untroubled
by cars, content to drowse in the
long sunny afternoons of Edwardian
England when Middlesex was still
rural.

Turn-of-the-century print of
Pinner church and nearby cottages.
While praising the delights of the
old church, the early guide went on
to point out that 'within its bound-
aries, Pinner has many dwellings of
modern type, and as a residential
district is becoming popular'. It
was also a favourite place for
school treats.

The south Hertfordshire district
south and west of Rickmansworth
has been worked for its gravel and
sand throughout the twentieth century, and early steam excavators of
the type that were used so success-
fully a few years earlier to create
the Great Central Railway's line
into Marylebone can be seen
working the far side of the south
Rickmansworth gravel pits.

In the lower picture a line of
trucks, including some marked
'Metropolitan', are loading in the
contractor's special siding. The
material at this part of the site was
barrowed directly into the trucks
from the excavations at the side,
while other planks were used to
level flush the loaded wagon.

A 'Bottom' near Chorley Wood. This pastoral scene was selected for reproduction in colour in a *Metro-land* guide – the outstanding achievement of the publication in days when colour reproduction was difficult and expensive.

Great Missenden farm. Past these lovely rural buildings, tricked out by the sun as it slipped between the deep shades of giant elms, strode the droves of adventurous Londoners, armed with the *Metro-land* walking guides to the Chiltern Hills. Walking caught the imagination of the public during the 1930s, as the popular music hall song 'I'm happy when I'm hiking' showed. It remained an important part of English recreational life.

A traditional scene of winter ploughing in the Chilterns, possibly taken on the slopes below Little Hampden. The plough also seems to be primitive, and this could be a publicity shot for the simple life. Horse ploughing was, of course, in general use in the 1930s, and very few 'Fordson' tractors challenged the noble animals.

Out in the now vanished Middlesex countryside, a train of Metropolitan saloon stock, headed by one of the 1926 experimental motor cars, pauses for the cameraman. This train was often kept for excursion traffic.

Quainton village, with its windmill and tumbledown cottages, was an ideal subject for the cameraman in his quest to popularize the attractions of the Chiltern Hills and the Vale of Aylesbury in the long-running series of *Metro-land* guides.

Pullman car 'Galatea' in original livery. The two Metropolitan Pullman cars were finished in full Pullman livery, and the interiors were finished in eighteenth-century style, with mahogany finish with inlaid woods in one car and oak in the other. The cars were fitted with end doors which were never used. The lavatory was kept locked out of use in the tunnels south of Finchley Road. The cars provided the buffet service which the Metropolitan Railway felt was necessary to avoid loss to the Great Central Railway of first class traffic over the outer areas.

This 'G' class locomotive (built by the Yorkshire Engine Co. in 1915) was named after the Metropolitan's dynamic general manager, Robert H. Selbie. He came from the Lancashire & Yorkshire Railway to the Metropolitan in 1903 as secretary, becoming general manager in 1908. His flare for innovation and publicity made 'Metro-land' a household word by the 1920s. His Metropolitan Railway Country Estates Company created the housing estates in Middlesex and the Chilterns that created much of the Met's traffic. Selbie died suddenly in 1930, at a time when Herbert Morrison's proposals for a London Passenger Transport Board were being discussed. Selbie wanted the Metropolitan to remain a 'main line', and it is said that he approached the Great Western Railway for a possible takeover. With Selbie gone, the Metropolitan's cause as a special case was lost.

This locomotive was sold (with other larger Metropolitan engines) to the LNER in 1937 and became 6155 (9076 after 1946). She ended her life in the Nottingham area in 1947-8.

The heart of Metro-land in 1906.
This view of the wide village street at Wendover, quite without cars or even traps, was common in the days before the First World War. A group of villagers, including a lady dressed in the most elegant of contemporary fashions, stand languidly outside the Red Lion Hotel, a popular place for Londoners to stay overnight on weekend rambling trips.

It was to this inn that Robert Louis Stevenson repaired while on his walk across the Chilterns in the 1890s from Wycombe to Tring, anticipating the wanderings of the poet Rupert Brooke. Stevenson, who had described his sylvan dream of the Chiltern Hills in *Autumn Effect*, had descended nearby Coombe Hill (then without its monument) and spent the night at the Red Lion, where his roving eye rested playfully on the landlord's daughter.

This impression of Brill comes from one of the earliest *Metro-land* guides and was, as the author instructs us, included as an up-to-date reminder of the beauty of the many lovely 'old worlde' villages that lie within reach of the Metropolitan Railway's fast, efficient service. Brill, of course, lay at the extreme end of the system, after a change at Quainton Road. Although the Met had arranged to take over the line on 1 December 1899, over five years later the little branch was still referred to in the company literature as the 'Oxford & Aylesbury Tramway'.

For those Londoners who could afford it, the ideal way to see the beauty of the Chiltern Hills in Edwardian days was to take a train from Baker Street to one of the faraway stations such as Great Missenden or Chesham. Here, if you were not able to mount your bike and did not feel inclined to 'heigh-ho' over the nearest stile and set out on foot, it was possible to take a conducted drive. At Chesham, these drives by waggonette departed on Wednesdays and Sundays throughout the season for such rural delights as Lee (near the home of the Liberty family) and Cholesbury. From Great Missenden, as this illustration shows, Mr L.C. Johnson would arrange for you to leave by a light trap or, more sedately, by waggonette. The main attraction here was a jog up the ridges to see the brand new South African War Monument on Coombe Hill, with a lovely leafy trot through the tall beechwoods where the trees split the afternoon sunlight into a weaving pattern of gold, so beautifully captured on the covers of *Metro-land* guides. The visitor was urged to look out for the simple country wood-worker – the bodger – carving chair legs deep in the woods. A simple sign that such an elfin character was around was, according to this guide, the telltale piles of turnings that would be fashioned into chairs, ready for transport by carrier's waggon or by train.

This rather faded old print is a reminder of the commercial possibilities of the White Lion livery stables at Great Missenden. Here you could hire a horse if you had failed to bring your own by Met from Finchley Road station, the London loading point.

The views of the rural Arcadia which tantalized the casual readers of the *Metro-land* guides of the 1920s and 1930s. As the years went by, the theme of these remarkable guides was increasingly upon the delights of simple, healthy country dwellers, living in houses built by the Metropolitan Estates Company on conveniently sited land close to the Metropolitan Railway, yet with views such as these within easy reach. The scenes around Rickmansworth, including these in the Loudwater House parkland, developed this idea without too much concern for the loss of such beauty which the estates themselves caused. As others took up the idea of mass building outside London by the early 1930s, the *Metro-land* guides were at last sounding notes of warning – at Pinner, for instance, the anonymous author noted: 'The woodman's axe has been ruthlessly swung here among the giant elms which are still a beautiful feature of Pinner's environment; those who lay out building estates ought to spare every fine tree they can.' The Met's estates, with houses appealing more to the well to do, could afford the benefits of good architects and careful landscape planning.

The Met's advertising extended to its envelopes! This printed promotion appeared on the 1932 envelopes used by the company.

2-6-4 tank locomotive No.114, the last class of engine built by the Met, at work here with wagons in Aylesbury sidings on 10 October 1925.

The Met's electric locomotives, with *Oliver Goldsmith* in the foreground, on 6 May 1933 at Neasden awaiting the last days of the independent Metropolitan Railway, then only weeks away. In spite of the rather unkempt side paint on this locomotive, most of the Metropolitan Railway stock continued to be well-maintained and resplendent until the final take-over.

This view of Neasden dates from about 1932. The poster to the left of the station entrance advertises the *Sunday Referee* . . . 'Good News From Germany'.

Bowers of Ruislip were building houses around the £1000 mark close to the village centre in 1932. The design was typical of the standard of the houses advertised in Metro-land guides.

Before Deciding—
visit Croft Estate, Ruislip

BUILT BY BOWERS

Superior Well - Built Detached and Semi-Detached Houses with accommodation for garages are now being erected at Croft Estate from £985 freehold, inclusive of all law costs, main drainage, company's water, electricity, gas services and complete with all labour saving equipment. Croft Estate is situate in the delightful old world village of Ruislip with its woodlands, commons, lakes and farm land surroundings and yet within a few minutes' walk of station and shops.

Terms arranged to individual requirements.

Call or 'phone— **H. L. BOWERS, Builder,**
Croft Estate Office, Ruislip
facing Metropolitan Station, frequent trains Baker Street (25 mins.) and City.
Telephone : Ruislip 217.

SAY YOU SAW IT IN "METRO-LAND."

ILLETT'S "*QUALITY*" HOUSES

EASONABLE in cost yet vastly superior, to many offered at a higher price, Gillett's houses, ...pily placed on Kenton's highest ...nt, will undoubtedly appeal. They ...built up to a standard and not down ...price; they represent the successful ...come of a keen endeavour to satisfy ...ry need, and everything likely to ...n labour and increase home comfort ...be found in their design.

The prices range from £1,045 to £1,525 and only superior materials and conscientious workmanship have been employed. Each house has a good garden and liberal frontage; each house a spacious garage or room for one. Their situation is both exclusive and accessible, and on the estate is a splendid club house with 22 tennis courts, whilst an 18-hole golf course adjoins the station.

Why not write, 'phone or call today for a copy of our "Houses of distinction" booklet describing the houses in detail —it will be well worth your while.

GEO. H. GILLETT & Co. Ltd.

Telephone - - Harrow 2514

Woodcock Hill Lane, Kenton, Harrow

Page 119

The Barn Hill Estate at Wembley was centred on the Preston Road station, which at the time was still very rural. A large stretch of land was purchased by the local council as a public park – a fact listed as an extra attraction to prospective house buyers, along with the inevitable golf and tennis clubs.

BARN HILL ESTATE WEMBLEY PARK

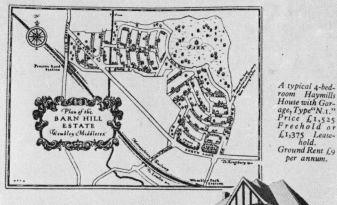

A typical 4-bedroom Haymills House with Garage, Type "N.1." Price £1,525 Freehold or £1,375 Leasehold. Ground Rent £9 per annum.

280 feet above Sea Level

Situated on the Southern and Western slopes of Barn Hill in the health-giving air of the open country, Barn Hill Estate has rapidly developed into one of the most attractive and convenient residential estates in N.W. London. More than 1,000 detached houses containing 3, 4 or 5 bedrooms are being built.

44 acres have been purchased by the Wembley Council for a Public Park. Every house will have a good garden back and front and space for a garage. Shops are already open on the estate. Golf and Tennis Clubs are within easy reach.

10 minutes from Baker Street

Wembley Park and Preston Road stations (Metro. Rly.) adjoin the Estate. The new arterial road affords motorists direct communication with London and all parts of the country.

Rates 4/9 in the £ for half-year. Main drainage. Colne Valley Company's water.

Visit Barn Hill Estate

and inspect the houses in course of construction. The Estate Office is 280 yds. from Wembley Park Stn. (turn left) and representatives are in constant attendance, including Saturdays and Sundays.

Gas and Electric light to all rooms. Interior decorations finished to purchaser's choice.

Prices from **£1,125 to £2,000**
(Leasehold and Freehold)
Building Society Mortgages arranged for 90% of the purchase price.

Write or 'phone for Booklet "C"

giving particulars, plans and prices of the various types of Houses being erected, and other most useful information. Free on request.

HAYMILLS, LTD.

1, GRAND PARADE
Forty Lane, Wembley Park
Telephone : Wembley 1736.

HAYMILLS HOUSES

Woodcock Hill, Kenton was another good quality area of new housing, built by Gillett, costing well over a thousand pounds for the superior semi-detached structure shown here. They were put up on the highest part of the district. The nearest stations were Preston Road or Northwick Park.

The Chesham shuttle in the last days of the Met: No. 80, a 0-4-4 T of the busy 'E' class working bunker forward on to the main line just outside Chalfont & Latimer station, with the three coaches of Dreadnought stock forming the 10.56 a.m. departure from Chesham on 5 June 1933.

After running round for the next trip, No. 80 is ready with her charges to meet passengers for Chesham from Baker Street on the same morning. The long rakes of freight wagons was a common sight at Chalfont in the dominant years of 'King Coal'.

Class 'F' locomotive No. 93 waits at Neasden with the breakdown crane train on 6 May 1923. There were four of these 0-6-2 tank locomotives, which were built in 1901 to deal with general freight duties on the main line to Verney Junction. During those years a considerable effort was made to increase freight on the railway, as the proportion of freight to passenger traffic compared unfavourably with other main line railways of the time.

The locomotives of the railway were resplendent in the deep crimson of the company, and were well maintained in clean condition during the 1920s. An illustration of the breakdown crane in action appears in *Romance of Metro-land*.

North Harrow, which was opened in 1915 at a spot near the old hamlet of Hooking Green, though the area did not develop until after the First World War. This picture was taken in about 1927 from the 'up' or Baker Street platform, and shows the old ticket hut. The con-fectioners and tobacconist kiosk adds an air of suburbia, although it is rather unhygenically sited as part of the station toilet building. Across the road, the Headstone Hotel is nearing completion with its 'billiard hall, dance hall and multiple bars for all classes'.

0-6-4 T Class 'G' locomotive *Robert
H. Selbie* entering Chalfont &
Latimer station with the 10.56 a.m.
train from Wendover to Baker
Street on 5 June 1933.

A much photographed locomotive, Class 'F' No. 93, heads an 'up' freight on 6 May 1933, only a few weeks before the end of the Metropolitan Railway. The gleam of the pipes and the general lustre of the dark crimson paintwork shows the great pride that the crews had in their stock right to the end.

Local carrier's wagon, about 1919.
This carter carried miscellaneous
parcels and wares around the
Buckinghamshire villages of Long
Crendon, Thame and into Aylesbury, and is typical of the local
horse-drawn services of the day.
Such a man would also have been
employed to move furniture.

6
Grandfather's Day
1933 to 1963
From the end of the Met
to the end of steam

With the birth of the London Passenger Transport Board in July 1933 the handsome locomotives of the 'K' class (Nos. 114 and 116 already appear earlier in this book) were repainted, along with the other locomotives, with the London Transport lettering. They continued their duties, dealing with freight and passengers working up to Verney Junction. Just before the day of the takeover, two locomotives (Nos. 91 and 105) had received an abbreviated 'MET' on the tanks, presumably as an economy measure.

Sketch of the Crown Inn at Amersham. Old Amersham has long been a favourite starting point for walks in the Chiltern Hills, and from early Metro-land days the well-worn path from the station through Lodge Wood to the old town offered the first glimpse of real countryside. The old town was noted for its attractive inns, with their gaily swinging signs, and the little teashops which can still be found there today.

LOOKING FOR A HOUSE?
TRY RICKMANSWORTH

In this region of green hillsides and woods, houses and sites are plentiful. To and from Rickmansworth, Chorley Wood, Croxley Green and Moor Park through trains run at short intervals. List of estate agents and builders from

'LONDON TRANSPORT', 55, BROADWAY, S.W.1

VICtoria 6800

See more of the country by living on the

E1/650

Building in Metro-land. Just because an Act of Parliament had created the new authority was no reason for the railway to stop encouraging new residents into Metro-land. This London Transport advertisement, one of the earliest issued by the new body, is quick to combine the ideals of a 'home of your own' (with all its idealistic pleasures of pushing lawn-mowers and gardening, with practical help in the form of Estate Agents' lists and season ticket rates – the eternal subject of railway advertising).

An Aylesbury train waiting at Baker Street while the crew takes a break between turns of duty. In Metropolitan days the same crews manned the same locomotive, No. 19, *John Wycliffe*, which came to an end on 31 December 1945 when it struck the rear of a T stock train near Northwood in thick fog. In the resulting fire three passengers lost their lives in the local train. No. 19 never returned to duty and was officially withdrawn from service on 12 March 1948.

– best beech woods,' said the Squirrel solemnly, 'best under the sun. If you've nothing else on hand, you two, this morning, I should like to take you round my little place down there. My beech leaf was never greener than this year's crop, never more incandescent.'

'Good spot, the Chilterns—

Near Chalfont and Latimer Station, on the Metropolitan Line, are Ladies' Arbour, West Wood and Park Wood. Together they form a great tract of beeches on a ridge, with footpaths threading its whole length. Cheap return tickets to the Chiltern country are issued, daily, from all stations on the Metropolitan and East London Lines. On Sundays and Bank Holidays by all trains. Mondays to Fridays between 10 and 4. Saturdays by all trains after 10. Chalfont and Latimer station (return fare 2/9) is 39 minutes from Baker Street (Metropolitan Line) or Marylebone (L.N.E.R.) Stations.

AWAY BY METROPOLITAN

LONDON TRANSPORT

FIN 357

In 1936 the London Passenger Transport Board ran a series of press advertisements emphasizing the attractions of the Chilterns under the banner 'Away by Metropolitan'. These featured lunatic animals that appeared embarrassingly before matchstick people, and told of the delights to be found from named stations on the line.

– though I know the place is my home,' said the Donkey, 'and I love my own juicy hedgerow there. But, frankly, is there anywhere a view more glorious, more stirring, than from the top of Bacombe Hill and Coombe Hill on a clear Spring day? Is there?'

'Good spot, the Chilterns—

Bacombe Hill begins near Wendover Station, on the Metropolitan Line, and rises gradually until it reaches Coombe Hill, the headland which, at 852 feet, is the highest point in the Chilterns. Cheap return tickets to the Chiltern country are issued, daily, from all stations on the Metropolitan and East London Lines. On Sundays and Bank Holidays by all trains. Mondays to Fridays between 10 and 4. Saturdays by all trains after 10. The return fare to Wendover Stn. is 4/3 from Baker Street (Metropolitan) or Marylebone (L.N.E.R.) Stations. **AWAY BY METROPOLITAN**

LONDON TRANSPORT

FIN 360

On the same theme, with copy by
Bryce Beaumont, came hints of
strange characters that one could
expect to meet on a day out in
Metro-land. Aimed at selling
cheap tickets to the Extension Line
stations, it demanded a working
knowledge of Latin; perhaps the
average Londoner already knew
enough about the Chilterns, so the
advertisement could be aimed at
visiting Cambridge dons. The vicar
in this advertisement appeared to
have much trouble with his dog-
collar – was that, perhaps, an
unconscious cry to be free?

HE came walking towards me through the beech trees. I got
up from the grass and asked him the time. He eased his collar,
looked at his watch and told me that it was hot.
'I find your country amazingly beautiful', I said.
'Indeed?' said the Vicar, prodding the edge of the path
with his stick, ' But then I find that most people like it !'
Behind him I could see the green curve of the land aquiver
with the wind in the wheat. He shrugged his shoulders and
turned to look at the hills.
' I don't know what it is about the Chilterns,' I said : ' it's
something in the freshness, the greenness of it all and the
way the skies hang over the fields. Surely you must see
all this ?'
' We're both biased', he said, after a pause. ' You, because
you are accustomed to street-enclosed skies and the freshness
of all this cannot but make you like it. I, because'—he
paused a moment—'because I have so grown into this country
that now I think it perfect'.
  He smiled and added, ' An qui amant ipsi sibi somnia fingunt'.
Then he dug his finger in his collar again and made off over
the hill.

Cheap day return tickets to the Chiltern country are issued from all Underground stations on the Metropolitan and East London Lines, daily. Sundays and Bank Holidays by all trains. Mondays to Fridays between 10 and 4. Saturdays by all trains after 10. Here (on right) are the return fares from Baker Street Station (Metropolitan Line) and from Marylebone Station (L.N.E.R.).	RICKMANSWORTH	2/3
	CHORLEY WOOD	2/6
	CHALFONT AND LATIMER	2/9
	CHESHAM	3/3
	AMERSHAM	3/-
	GT. MISSENDEN	3/8
	WENDOVER	4/3
	STOKE MANDEVILLE	4/6

Good Spot, the Chilterns

LONDON TRANSPORT

E2N.542

**Early London Transport advertise-
ments** for the Chilterns later
broadened in appeal, as these 1937
advertisements show. The new
authority had to bring the widest
volume of pleasure traffic to the
Chilterns, in accordance with the
policy of the time of filling seats
during 'off-peak' times and especially at weekends. Green Line as
well as Metropolitan Line services
were featured and advertisements
were placed with care according to
the readership.

  These were the days of Ravilious's
delightful woodcuts, which remained a feature of London
Transport *Country Walks* books
until the mid 1970s. These delightful scraperboard headings
representing idealized activities of
this rural arcadia, remain some of
the most remarkable expressions
of early London Transport art to
appear in the mid 1930s. Of
course, the cross-cut saw and the
funny old shepherd were seldom to
be seen, even in those days.

The Chilterns are remarkable for the many fine views over the Vale of Aylesbury. This path, gouged deep into the chalk, leads up to Bacombe Hill from the far side of the Wendover monument.

Things are not what they were, nor ever will be; but the sun still warms the face of the old inn, where grandad (like his father before him) shakes his head over the crops, bemoans the rabbits and the price of wheat, raises his mug to 'The King, God bless 'un.'

Green Line for

Green Line for *'Ope an' Anchor*

Open Air

J.S. O'Connor's sketch here encapsulates the attraction of walking in the Chilterns before the Second World War. Canny old characters could still be found to spin a yarn or two for incredulous Londoners as they paused to consult their maps and take some refreshment. One of the most remote old inns was the Leather Bottle, near Wendover, which served beer from the barrel in the front room of a tiny cottage.

Rowland Hilder's dreamy look at Metro-land in the low evening sun of those Sundays of the 1930s is perhaps romantic, but it is in keeping with days filled with happiness, of impromptu cricket matches with the children on grassy, sloping 'pitches', of wasps around the picnic basket, the sight of horses ploughing, and of watching the cleanly cut sheaves of corn being stacked in groups for the farm cart at harvest time. Now the giant elms and the haycart have gone.

Hilder was born in 1905 in Long Island. A contemporary of Rex Whistler, he learned engraving alongside Sutherland at Goldsmiths'. All these artists were to be commissioned, with Ravilious and Edward Bawden, to work on London Transport publicity. Hilder was to say of landscape work years later: 'All of a sudden, you see something which makes you catch your breath. You go back to find it and it's all gone. In fact, it's inside you. I try to put it together by using all the technique I can summon up.'

BUCKINGHAMSHIRE

The green Chilterns moulded with beech woods look down on drowsy villages and gardens aglow with hollyhocks. And old towns, like Amersham and Beaconsfield, are gay with swinging signs. South are the cool depths of Burnham Beeches, where the forest path leads to shadowed quiet. And it is country for those who like to walk in the solitude of open fields.

Beaconsfield

By Green Line route Q daily from Oxford Circus (Upper Regent Street). Coaches run every hour (half-hourly on Saturday afternoons and Sundays). Return fare 3/-.

Amersham

By Green Line route R daily from Oxford Circus (Upper Regent Street) or route B daily from Victoria (Eccleston Bridge). Coaches run every hour on each route, on Saturday afternoons and Sundays every half-hour on route R. Return fare 3/3.

Burnham Beeches

By Green Line route P on Saturday afternoons and Sundays from Whitehall (Horse Guards Avenue). Coaches run every half-hour. Return fare 3/6.

Wendover

By Green Line route B daily from Victoria (Eccleston Bdge). Hourly. Return fare 4/-.

Chalfont St. Giles

By Green Line route R daily from Oxford Circus (Upper Regent Street). Coaches run every hour, on Saturday afternoons and Sundays half-hourly. Return fare 3/-.

LONDON TRANSPORT 55 BROADWAY SW1 VICTORIA 6800

E2N.317.37

Shardoloes

Shardoloes, set amid the contrary waters of the Misbourne, was viewed by a number of paths which remain to be used today. Its white stuccoed Georgian front could be seen from the carriages of the Metropolitan train as it made its way from Amersham to Great Missenden. It survives today in the form of independent flats. This, and the sketch of the Crown (page 102), are by the authors.

A freight train waits, with steam up, beyond the short semaphore signal at Great Missenden in this early 1960s view.

To REACH ANY PART OF LONDON QUICKLY , AND IN COMFORT, TRAVEL FROM CROXLEY GREEN OR WATFORD STATIONS
(LONDON TRANSPORT & L·N·E·R)

Through Electric Trains run to and from the City throughout the day. At Baker Street and Marylebone the train services connect with the **UNDERGROUND** for West End.

Cheap Day Tickets at about the single fare for the return journey are issued to Baker Street and Marylebone and all London and Suburban stations on the Metropolitan Line, Weekdays after 10 a.m., Sundays by all trains. Cheap Day Tickets are issued similarly to stations between Harrow and Verney Junction on Wednesdays and Saturdays after 10 a.m., Sundays by all trains (except stations closed on Sundays).

Quarterly, Monthly and Seven-day Season Tickets and Workmen's Tickets are available.

A frequent Service of Buses runs between Watford Station and the High Street, Watford.

Press advertisement of 1937 to encourage use of the Watford service.

The Brill Branch was one of the first casualties of the new London Passenger Transport Board. After an official inspection of the branch, it was announced that the line would close – the last day being 30 November 1935. Those cameramen who visited the branch before its end captured some exciting glimpses of the real rural simplicity of a country railway where that usually most important of all things, the timetable, was relatively unimportant. This and some of the following views of the Brill Branch have been published in the past, but are shown here as a reminder of those days.

The level crossings were a feature of the Brill Branch. No statutory powers had been sought or obtained for these crossings, the most important of which allowed the railway across the A41 Bicester – Aylesbury road at Waddesdon. After the Board of Trade inspection of October 1894 they were approved by the county council, subject to the normal position of the gates being against the tramway. This crossing could have been seen near Quainton Road junction.

The Brill Branch line ran quite straight after leaving Quainton Road until it reached the main Bicester Road. The track appears in this picture to be well used as it ran between hedges, with the small country road from Quainton just over to the left. This is today the clearest feature of the old railway, which otherwise left hardly a trace, even in 1960 when the authors walked the original route.

The old rigid eight-wheeled carriage of 1866 used on the Brill line, which ran on the very last afternoon of the passenger service in 1935. It is seen here at Quainton Road in that year, having recently been repainted in London Transport livery.

The same coach at Brill station in 1934. Note the wooden planking that formed the platform.

Another view of Brill during the last years. Here locomotive No. 23, one of the two 'service' locomotives used on the branch, has 'run round' and awaits the necessary pressure of steam before taking the train back to Quainton Road.

This photograph of the goods shed at Brill station is far from perfect; it has been included to show the north side of the building and the doors covering the ramp, with the cart track in the foreground leading to the road.

The crossing of the Great Central Railway at Wotton, 1935. This was one of the few examples of double track work on the Brill Branch. The Brill Branch lines sweep in from the left, and are duplicated to allow by-pass to be achieved. The lines led, leftwards, to Wotton station, where there was a goods siding. The bricks for this bridge were made at the Brill brickworks, and transported by the old tramway.

This is the classic view of the Brill train taken in the most picturesque part of the track, which ran through light woodland between Wotton and Wood Siding. No. 23 heads the train. This was the easiest part of the line to return to nature, and years later not a bolt or spike of metal from this track bed could be found.

The goods shed and platform at Wotton. In addition to the siding in the foreground there was another siding, which ran off the main line just beyond the platform and ran beside the line of trees in the back-ground. A considerable number of passengers await the train – perhaps a token of its approaching retire-ment. This view is taken from the east side; the Great Central bridge lay behind the camera.

No. 41 arrives with the train from Quainton Road at Brill in the Summer of 1935. Alighting passengers passed down the ramp to the ticket collector cum station-master, a position offered to Metropolitan Railway staff on seniority.

During the last week, the LNER notice board (here displaying an advertisement for dining car services featuring an eighteenth-century character in an advanced state of intoxication) was removed with other station fixtures. Much

of this material was sold. (See also photograph in the companion volume *Metro Memories*.)

Brill had little to offer the visitor apart from its charm and some wonderful views after a steep climb to the village from the station. There is still a windmill on Brill Hill, which was in working order until 1968 and is still well cared for. The last miller was Albert Nixey, who used the mill for rough grinding until 1916. For many years the village had two mills, the earliest of which, built in 1634, was pulled

down (or rather fell down) in 1906.

The only way to reach Brill by rail after the demise of the Met was to travel to Brill & Luggershall station and walk an extra mile or so. By 1938, when a traveller did this, he found villagers 'looking harder at me than anyone in wildest Wales or Lakeland would have done'. He reported that upon reaching the site of Brill station he found the white crossing gate still there, but the track 'guiltless of sleepers', and masses of undergrowth was half-choking the oil-laden stones.

Brill station, looking east in summer 1934, with No. 23, smartly tricked out in London Transport livery, ready to leave for Quainton Road. This picture gives a clear view of the engine shed and water tower, as well as the track arrangement.

No. 41, working at Brill in 1933. This picture shows the miscellaneous station buildings, including the engine shed and the brick workshop which was as tumbledown inside as it appears from the outside. Here small repairs could be made with the aid of the small furnace.

L44, the old Met locomotive No. 1 (the original No. 1 was, of course, a Beyer Peacock 0-4-4T, but was scrapped after being involved in an accident).

Locomotive L44, with renovated milk van No. 3 and compartment stock during celebrations in 1963. At the turn of the century even a station as close to London as Willesden Green had its own Milk Dock at the end of Platform 4, in that case.

Reminders of the past in the ground: the line of the old track-way leading to Wotton Green, once used by the Brill Branch trains. The raised surface and hedge lines still hint of the past.

No. 41272 at Chalfont & Latimer
Station, with the Chesham shuttle
stock, as a London-bound train
prepares to leave, 1960.

No. 41272, one of the providers of steam power north of Rickmansworth at the time, at work with the Ashbury coaches of the Chesham shuttle in the attractive countryside above Chesham. In the second photograph she is at work tender forwards on the return to Chesham in 1960.

Locomotive No. 9, *John Milton*, at rest outside the Neasden Engine sheds on 15 September, 1934. You may just glimpse her sister locomotive *Benjamin Disraeli* behind her.

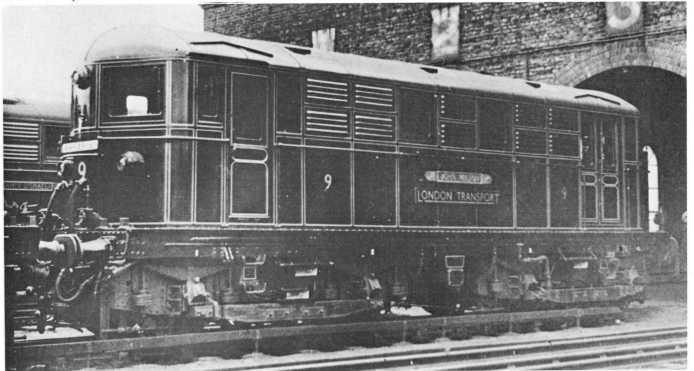

Bus services were surprisingly good in the 1930s, and villages in the Misbourne Valley like Chalfont St Giles relied on the village bus to connect with the nearest railway station or town. As this picture shows, private cars were few, and this was ideal walking country. During the 1930s there was considerable alarm caused by the lack of water in the Misbourne, which has a tendency to 'disappear' below into the chalk. The old stories had it that the Misbourne ran dry to foretell times of trouble and disaster ahead.

The service between Aylesbury and Verney Junction was run by a LNER Railmotor coach during the last years of passenger working. This is the view at Granborough Road station during the last summer, 1936, as Railmotor GER 242 Tank 8307 releases some surplus steam and gets ready to leave.

In Edwardian days, anyone living at Verney Junction could take a through rail excursion to Margate, Broadstairs or Ramsgate. It was all Met stock, leaving Verney Junction at 5.18 a.m. and returning from Ramsgate at 7.25 p.m.

Granborough Road almost forty years later – on 9 March 1974. Soft meadow grasses blow over the platforms, and the track has been used as a line for power cables.

Another view of Granborough Road station – this time the service is in the opposite direction. There was considerable freight traffic, especially the transport of cattle, from these stations during the days of the Metropolitan Railway.

Verney Junction on 9 August 1974. The main line track to Oxford is still in position, but the diesels run through a weed-strewn platform. The line to Baker Street left the double tracks in a curve to the right, close to the site of the low bungalow beyond the old station house.

Up the Junction – Verney Junction, terminus of the Metropolitan Railway, in March 1936, showing the Verney Yard Box, a wide spread of track, and beyond the signal a mixed freight train waiting on Verney Junction platform to enter the Bicester main line.

This beautifully restored third class carriage of so-called Ashbury stock was of the type used on the suburban lines after electrification, and, in London Transport days, ran as steam stock between Chalfont & Latimer and Chesham.

Uxbridge, Belmont Road, with one of the 'MV' type compartment stock trains, about 1933. The terminus was conveniently sited so that the line could be extended to Denham or even southwards to Windsor. The refreshment room at Uxbridge was well known for its cleanliness and was in charge of a Mr and Mrs Moss. Their home-cooked ham rolls were a speciality. In winter Mr Moss would replenish the refreshment room fire with coal every quarter of an hour.

Another picture of Belmont Road, Uxbridge, with one of the 'bogie' stock trains on the right. The leading vehicle is a control trailer, the motor car being at the other end. The picture dates from about 1933. The train on the left is on the Piccadilly Tube service, extended from South Harrow on 23 October 1933. The Underground Group under Frank Pick had been a byword for good design and particularly for the quality of its signs, so we can suppose that the station staff at Uxbridge got into trouble about the local press report of a scruffy, badly hung canvas sign announcing: 'Through trains now running to Piccadilly and the West End. Single fare Leicester Square 1/7d.'

Northwood's main shopping centre at Green Lane, November 1934. On the left is the Northwood Hotel, demolished in the early 1960s. Northwood was the earliest suburb to develop on the Extension Line. The first fifty plots of land were offered in 1887, when the station opened. A visitor recalled: 'At a forty-minute ride from Town on the Metropolitan Extension (fare 1/6d) stands the village or hamlet of Northwood and in a quiet mile from this is the grand new station in all the gloss of gleaming new paint and fresh gravel . . . there's not a house in view from the platforms.' Even in 1921 the district was said to be 'completely cut off by long stretches of truly rural and beautiful countryside . . . late trains are specially run for theatregoers.' The trains included one of the Met's famous Pullman cars for those who liked extra comfort.

By the late 1930s advertising by the estate developers was more elaborate. The influence of the cinema is seen in this three-dimensional signboard in Swakeleys Road, Ickenham, by The Avenue: Dunster Richards are 'Presenting Lovely Milton Court' with houses from £895 to £1350. Ickenham Hall Estate was actually a good half mile from the ancient building of that name. There is a note of irony too. 'Procure while you can, houses of distinction and value'. A few months later Hitler invaded Poland and few people had time to think about a new home in Metroland.

Electric trains began running to Rickmansworth in January 1925 (the Watford branch opened in November of that year). A special press train was run early in January; the electric locomotive was No. 16, driven by Motorman Wiggins of Harrow. The train consisted of 'Dreadnought' carriages and the Rothschild Saloon, which had been specially built for Lord Rothschild of Halton (originally as two vehicles). 'We experienced neither jolt nor disturbance from start to finish,' wrote one reporter; 'a fine test of good driving and first class railway rolling stock.' The extension of electric lines from Harrow consumed 10,000 cable posts, 30,000 porcelain insulators, 4000 tons of conductor rails and 30,000 copper bonds; 60 colour light signals were installed and there were five new signal cabins fitted with illuminated traffic diagrams. The electric locomotive here, heading south with a rush hour train to the City, is *Benjamin Disraeli*.

The last days of Metro-land at Ruislip – October 1939. The sandbags have been filled and the ARP and Fire Service are ready at the top of St Martin's Approach. Now it's almost too late to 'Choose your own site in the beautiful woods and a house of distinction on an exclusive estate', being offered by A.V. Low at Park Avenue and Broadwood Avenue.

Although Ickenham Halt opened in 1905, there was no ticket hut till 1910. Even in 1971 passengers had to stand here in the street for their tickets. The telephone box came in 1926, the first public call box (except for the village Post Office) in the area.

Metropolitan Farewell: the last day of electric locomotive and steam-hauled trains, 9 September 1961. The scene here is at Rickmansworth and seldom can the platforms have been as crowded. No. 18 *Michael Faraday* was withdrawn on 7 March 1963 and later went (with Nos. 2, 7 and 16) to the English Electric Company at Rugby for use in tests.

Waddesdon Road, on the Brill Branch, on the last summer that the Metropolitan Railway ran to Brill. This photograph was taken on 8 April 1933 and shows how even the tiniest station had a siding for local coal traffic. The crossing at the Bicester – Aylesbury road is in the background. This station, originally Waddesdon, was renamed Waddesdon Road on 1 October 1922.

Most of the Met's steam locomotives had very long lives. The two 'F' class engines seen here with works trains at Harrow in May 1948 were built in 1901 by the Yorkshire Engine Company. They spent most of their lives working short goods trains. L51 (Met 92) and L50 (Met 91) were withdrawn in 1957 and 1958 respectively.

BRIEF TABLE OF
STATION NAME CHANGES ON THE EXTENSION LINE

Station	Became	Date
Waddesdon	Waddesdon Road	1 October 1922
Grandborough Road	Granborough Road	6 October 1920
(Quainton Road to Verney Junction converted to single track		28 January 1940)
Waddesdon Manor	Waddesdon	1 October 1922
Chalfont Road	Chalfont & Latimer	20 November 1915
Sandy Lodge	Moor Park & Sandy Lodge	until 18 October 1925
Moor Park & Sandy Lodge	Moor Park	25 September 1950
Kilburn Brondesbury	Kilburn	25 September 1950
St John's Wood Road	St John's Wood	1 April 1925
St John's Wood	Lords	11 June 1939 (closed 20 November that year)

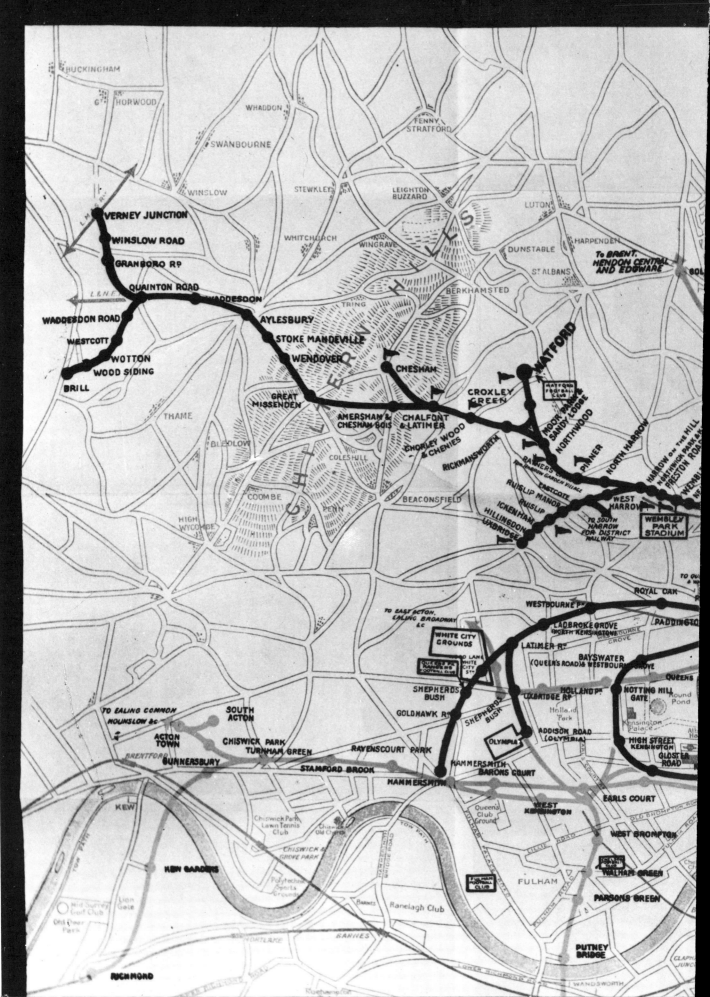